GAME URBANISM

Hans Venhuizen
GAME URBANISM
Manual for Cultural Spatial Planning

With contributions by
Charles Landry
Francien van Westrenen

VALIZ, Amsterdam

REASSURING END-PICTURES REMOVE ALL FEAR OF CHANGE

CULTURE

YET ALSO CURIOSITY
ABOUT AN UNCERTAIN RESULT

THE DESIRED INTERCHANGEABLE IDIOSYNCRASY

GUT

OVERSHADOWS THE IDIOSYNCRATIC NON-INTERCHANGEABILITY

A DYNAMIC

THE FIRST DESIGN OF
A PROCESS OF CHANGE

WITHOUT LIES

IS THE IDENTITY OF
THE PROCESS OF CHANGE ITSELF

**CULTURAL HISTORY IS
ONLY OF VALUE**

WHAT YOU WANT IT TO BE

IF THAT VALUE LIES
IN THE PRESENT

TODAY'S PROBLEMS

LIMITATIONS

PRODUCE TOMORROW'S ICONS

**STRONG IDENTITIES
ARE NOT NECESSARILY
PLEASANT OR CHARMING**

IS A VERB

AND CHIEFLY
EMERGE FROM
STRUGGLE AND GARBAGE

DESIGN

IN EVERY CONTEXT
THE PHENOMENA

THE COMMISSION

ARE WHAT SHAPE
AMBITION

THE BEST IDEA
IS INDEED ALWAYS

OF CHANGE

THE IDEA
YOU THINK OF YOURSELF

DOING-

THOUGH DOING-AS-IF

AS-IF

WERE NOT ALSO SIMPLY DOING

EVEN THE BEST
MASTER PLAN

MANAGER

ONLY WORKS WITH A PLAN MASTER

CONTENTS

PAGE

Charles Landry
THINK CULTURALLY, PLAN IMAGINATIVELY AND ACT ARTISTICALLY

Hans Venhuizen makes cultural planning seem so logical, straightforward and easy. It is as if over the last two decades there has been a seamless, obstacle free development of this concept of planning. The reality is far different. Getting the idea of cultural planning accepted has been a hard task, there has been resistance, and incomprehension as to what it is. And there is still a long way to go, but Hans is one of the few people who have been part of that struggle for a long time. Before we talk about him let us take a step back in time.

Where are we now: The word 'planning' as far as cities goes has for too long been concerned with the hardware of the city. It is still the default position. When you say the word 'planning' without a suffix like 'economic', 'social' or 'cultural' you immediately think of dividing up land uses, building roads, deciding where houses or other physical infrastructure are going to go. Most planners in cities have this type of physically oriented training in their background and the world outside thinks of planning in this way too. They are the people who 'won't allow me to build my extension'. These are the 'insensitive folks who let that ugly building be constructed in my town centre'. They are 'not resurfacing the road on my way to work'. Their control of the 'masterplan' reinforces these kinds of views; they also hold the central position and so dominate the two-dimensional world perspective. Planners have never been much loved. Yet there are many in the profession who have great values and who want the best for their communities. They understand the complexities of people and place. Yet somehow the 'system' turns them into something we do not like. The question is: is it the system or is it the way planners have been taught to think.

A couple of decades ago 'economic planning' gained dramatically in status as cities adjusted to the deep transformation brought about by the move from the industrial economy to one based more on services and knowledge intensity. This at least brought people into the picture, mainly those in business. This in turn fostered 'strategic planning'. This is where the 'clever guys' went who understood about the connection of things and who knew about things like vision, goals and objectives. Social planning was either seen as a form of social engineering to be avoided or as those 'people down the corridor dealing with all those problem families'. I exaggerate in my stereotyping, of course.

29

Tracing the past: The essence of what we now know as cultural planning, as Colin Mercer reminds us, was outlined long, long ago by Patrick Geddes (1854–1932), who was a Scottish biologist also known for his innovative thinking in the fields of urban planning and education. It is useful to remind ourselves of some of his principles elaborated, for instance, in *Cities in Evolution* (1915). All planning he asserted should take account of three core issues: folk, work and place. This implies that planners understand themselves as anthropologists, sociologists, historians, economists as well as geographers and not just experts in land uses. They need to know how people relate and experience their environment, what gives meaning to their lives and how they live, work and use their spare time. In effect he argues that planning not a physical science but a human science. Geddes insisted: 'Survey before plan' and he noted '...we must excavate the layers of our city downwards, into its earliest past...and thence we must read them upwards, visualising as we go.' He implies that we need to trace peoples' visions and values and integrate their intricate histories and memories of their urban environments into the planning process before we actually plan. This was visionary.

The routes of cultural planning: Cultural planning, to my knowledge, in the more modern sense was first used as a term in the 1980's. It always was a phrase people found difficult to understand. People interpreted it as planning for arts facilities like theatres or symphony halls or putting on a festival, but it always had a far broader scope. Partners for Liveable Communities (formerly Places) in Washington were the first organization to publicize the concept. They saw it as the planning of urban resources including design, architecture, parks, the natural environment, animation and especially arts activity within that and tourism. They were influenced by Wolf von Eckhardt, the architecture correspondent of the *Washington Post* who in 1980 in 'The Arts & City Planning' noted that 'effective cultural planning involves all the arts, the art of urban design, the art of winning community support, the art of transportation planning and mastering the dynamics of community development'. The terms were introduced into Europe by Franco Bianchini in 1990, who coming from Italy was acquainted with their notion of 'resorsi culturali', which had existed in Italy for over fifty years. He added to the definition by saying 'the art of forming partnerships between the public, private and voluntary sectors and ensuring the fair distribution of economic, social and cultural resources'. Colin Mercer took up the term in Australia in 1991 and noted that cultural planning has to be 'the strategic and integral use of cultural resources in urban and community development'. In particular he focused on the idea of cultural mapping. He added that planning should not be about producing and developing goods and commodities but be about developing people – citizens. This means 'relearning the civic arts of citizen-formation if we are to aim not just for 'urban' but for civic renewal'.

In a series of collaborative projects in the late 1980's and early 1990's Franco Bianchini and I also elaborated on the terms cultural planning and resources. We noted that you needed to plan cultural resources, which are embodied in peoples' creativity, skills and talents. They are not only 'things' like buildings, but also symbols, activities and the repertoire of local products in crafts, manufacturing and services. Urban cultural resources include the historical, industrial and artistic heritage representing assets including architecture, urban landscapes or landmarks. They include too: Local and indigenous traditions of public life, festivals, rituals or stories as well as hobbies and enthusiasms, which can exist simply for enjoyment, but they can also be rethought to generate new products or services. Resources like language, food and cooking, leisure activities, clothing and sub-cultures or intellectual traditions that exist everywhere are often neglected, but can be used to express the specialness of a location. And, of course, cultural resources are the range and quality of skills in the performing and visual arts and the creative industries. We stated: 'Cultural resources are the raw materials of the city and are its value base; its assets replacing coal, iron or gold. Creativity is the method of exploiting these resources and helping them grow. The task of urban planners is to recognize, manage and exploit these resources responsibly. An appreciation of culture should shape the technicalities of urban planning and development rather than being seen as a marginal add-on to be considered once the important planning questions like housing, transport and land-use have been dealt with. So a culturally informed perspective should condition how planning as well as economic development or social affairs should be addressed.' Cultural resources reflect where a place is, why it is like it is and where its potential might lead it. This focus draws attention to the distinctive, the unique and the special in any place.

In our naivety we thought these were clear statements and that the planning world would immediately be converted to cultural planning. How wrong we were. We did not appreciate the strength of the professions, how entrenched they were in their educational formation and how difficult it was for them to shift their mind and to look at things differently. To many cultural planning still seemed vague, going through the process takes too long, the outcomes are unclear. There was no compelling argument to take the ideas on board. The more traditional physical and economic planners contrasted this with their own approach that seemed to have tangible, often physical, outcomes and clear targets.

Progress has been made, however, and this is because the various disciplines involved in planning have begun to understand that appreciating the software of the city is as vital to success as is creating physical infrastructure. For this reason the concept of cultural planning in its fuller sense has emerged in the statutory literatures of a few places like the Netherlands or Australia. The disciplines involved in city-making recognized that the look and feel of the industrial city is different from one based on knowledge intensity or one where the city is there to create experiences. But the danger has always been that culture loses its depth, rich texture and complexity and is seen merely as art or as a method of beautifying places. It is still too often a marginal add-on brought in as an idea when the going gets tough in a development process. As someone once said to me: 'After a short dose of cultural planning, let's get down to the basics of development and then let the 'regen lads' take over'. These are the project managers who get rid of all the woolly stuff and focus again solely on the hardware of the city.

A final point: 'Cultural planning' is still a cumbersome term, it seems to imply specifically planning for culture and it sounds a touch dirigiste. It is in fact the opposite. It is a process of exploring, discovering and unleashing potential and letting that unfold through a paced and purposeful process where ideas or visions emerge that have cultural power. That is they have meaning and importance for those involved and concerned. Such visions are far more likely to generate the motivation, will and energy to create projects that sustain themselves over time, because they are organic, change over time and with circumstance. They are more likely to be adaptable and thus ultimately resilient.

A few words about me and my own experience: I have tried to apply cultural planning and cultural resource thinking to my work over many years. Thinking back I have failed more than I have succeeded. My first strategy was to argue for the arts and I undertook a raft of studies as to why the arts are important to city development. This was fine as far as it went. We talked a lot about the reasons why art was important, such as its role in challenging the status quo, in reminding us that issues of beauty and ugliness were important or that the arts can inspire and help self-expression. But issues like design and architecture or community arts continually upset the neat categories of the arts world. It did not quite do the trick. My second focus in the early 1980's was to highlight the importance of the cultural industries (later called the creative economy) covering areas from the music, design or film industries. This allowed me to link cultural activities to economic agendas and enabled me to get some traction with the planning community. Through this it was possible to link people to place and to explore what kind of places people wanted if they were to express themselves more fully. The idea of urban distinctiveness and being globally competitive played a key role in this. The threat of another city being interesting was always a way of getting the attention urban strategists and decision makers. Under this guise issues of identity and meaning could be slipped in. I explored this in a variety of cities from Glasgow, Birmingham, Barcelona, South Africa, St. Petersburg, and Cracow.

This approach reached its limits after some time. For me the notion of creativity kept on coming into play and I resisted the idea that the only creative people were those working with arts. Through my work I met many creative people involved in social affairs, business, the public administration or ordinary citizens. It reminded me that it was the way they addressed problems and discovered opportunities in a fluid, flexible and open minded manner that was powerful. I saw too how they instinctively thought about things in a cultural resources way – ranging over possibilities, looking at options, thinking about things afresh.

The impact of these encounters took me on a long trajectory and made me focus on the idea of the creative city. Within this concept I then folded in the idea of cultural planning. Creativity was something that everyone could relate to whether an economist, a physical planner or a social worker apart from artists and those involved in the creative industries. Practically every city in Europe has had to rethink what its role and purpose is in the new configuration. When I wrote the first shorter version of the creative city in 1995 (with Franco Bianchini) and then a far more extensive version in 2000 it seemed to touch a chord. Instead of doing work with culture, arts or heritage departments in local governments the focus shifted. We worked with strategy divisions concerned with the future of their city. Talking then about issues like culture, identity or the creativity of citizens or business was natural. They all seemed like urban assets to be explored. It was easier for people to recognize that there is more to a creative city than it being defined as a place with a strong arts and heritage fabric or one with a strong cultural economy or even a large creative class, which includes the former as well as the knowledge and research community. Instead I suggested that the creative city is a place that embeds a 'culture of creativity' in how it goes about its business. This means too that everyone is potentially creative and that it can come from any source. Cultural resources thinking can neatly interweave its way into this discussion and strategy making process. I have had the opportunity to explore and talk about this approach in a number of cities like Bilbao, Adelaide, Perth, Helsinki, across Asia and North America and even small cities in Albania.

Clearly the word 'creativity' is in danger of being overused and so its meaning can hollow out and become empty. It remains important whatever. The first task though, like Hans exemplifies so well, is to encourage curiosity, from that it then possible to trigger the imagination. With imagination it is possible to generate creative ideas and solutions from which new concepts, approaches or inventions can emerge. If they are applied they then become innovations. Enough of me now.

Reflecting on everything I think the term 'planning culturally' or 'planning creatively' is better than 'cultural planning'. It implies that we have cultural literacy and that it is possible to use the resources of the imagination. This brings me back to Hans Venhuizen.

Hans thinks culturally. He looks at places and asks: Where do they come from, where are they now, where could they be going and what could they become. He understands that in a location or place, whether this is a constructed landscape, a city, a neighbourhood, a newly built school, a motorway or a garage it is the embodied culture that shapes and determines the potential. This culture is a double-edged sword for places in development. Sometimes the culture constrains and holds back, because people only see what was with rose tinted glasses without perhaps remembering the darker sides and unexplored stories. But even where people want to keep things as they are or be nostalgic that is a form of development too. The resulting physical presence of things left the same and the mental attitudes and activities that go with them lead down a development path. Those with an appreciation of cultural literacy can immediately decode and understand the results. At times this leads to lifelessness.

Alternatively unpacking the culture can open up a treasure trove of forgotten stuff. It can remind people of why things are as they are and why they came about. It can make people look more closely and attentively both at the detail and the broad sweep of how things connect historically and today. It can teach people to feel the presence of their surroundings more emotionally and viscerally in an unmediated way. It can help people sense the resonance of a place at a higher and deeper register of experience. This can trigger links and associations and so encourage people to play with the past, present and futures. In some instances it is known to have healed people's mental landscape, because they understand better who they are and why.

Hans sees culture as a resource and with this approach everything and everyone can become relevant at any given moment. It is not only the past etched into the physical although this can be important. It is also what people do and how they think. He looks closely and with an open, inquisitive mind at topography, architecture or old or neglected structures that lie forlorn in the landscape looking for a new purpose. He considers too what products and services evolved, which skills were involved and whether they could be reused for today. He looks at traditions and contemporary forms of social life and assesses the mainstream as well as alternative culture because he knows that within the counter culture the new culture is being born.

Hans is like a surveyor of possibility and as he says the first step in the work is like going on an expedition and this reminds me of Patrick Geddes. The research has no simple objective in mind, but there is an intense desire to get there. You have to be continually alert, and prepared for unexpected twists and turns, you need to let yourself be surprised and confounded. You don't know what you will find. The process of discovery is unpredictable, but lessons are learnt along the way. In some cases the hidden and submerged can become vital, whilst the currently dominant things can reduce in importance. It is 360 degree thinking, holistic in scope and intention. This helps turn weaknesses into strength such as the project **AMPHIBIOUS LIVING**, which deals with water living or **ALLES WIRD GUT** that looks at the advantages of shrinkage or **THE PHENOMENAL ROAD** which seeks to get motorways to add to the landscape rather than detract from it. It can also mean the ability to see a planning task through a diversity of eyes like the young, the old, the business world or those that want calmness or those that want wildness. With this information at hand we suddenly have a plethora of opportunities.

AMPHIBIOUS LIVING
pp 73, 152-163

Working with cultural resources is inevitably a participative process. To discover the full range of local assets requires working with people grounded in their place and the project. The trick is to balance well the lack of knowledge or even ignorance and potential freshness and clarity of the outsider with the depth of understanding yet possible inability to see the wood for the trees of the insider. I think this is what Hans means when he talks of 'necessary distance' and 'involved proximity'. This works best when people trust, respect and even admire you. Hans has achieved this in many cases. But is has not been plain sailing. At last people are beginning to understand how to commission him because they know what he does.

Hans has a difficult job because he wants to change the way we think about planning, how we go about planning itself and ultimately how we do projects. He wants to bend the narrow logic of spatial, economic and social planning whose results increasingly disappoint and make people unhappy. He wants to release, emancipate and then nurture, support and give confidence to the imagination. In so doing he combines different disciplines in his teams, he involves communities, the varied interests of a place and many outside experts. It feels at times as if Hans is managing a football team of diverse skills, and his cultural-historical projects are good examples of this. It brings two worlds together, 'cultural history' and 'spatial planning' which have different methodologies, ways of looking and interpreting and different planning horizons.

Hans, I believe, likes the tension that thinking culturally engenders. He wants good dilemmas that are nearly irresolvable to create pressure. He wants to use this to raise standards and aspirations that often go against predominant grain. With the right supportive environment this can trigger the imagination and energy. Some of these dilemmas include: blending the old and the new in a way that satisfies both the preservationists who want to protect the existing environment and those who want the stylishly modern. The solution here cannot be a simple compromise or mediocrity. Instead it needs to drive deeper into desires. Both parties want a form of authenticity and going against the grain of the local culture helps discover what the contemporary version of this may be uncluttered by media images.

Another dilemma is to be stuck in patterns of thought. Here Hans uses paradox or contradiction to get the thinking going and to help people to jump out of their fixed mental framework.

Word play and metaphor are significant tools. For instance, in the LIMES project, to talk of 'the future of history' as Hans does reminds us that history is not a static thing where once and for all it was decided what the history of a neighbourhood was. There are layers of history and multiple interpretations and the play of power and interests obscures some aspects and highlights others. The LIMES project is a good example. To talk of a project in terms of the 'theatre of digging' not only brings to life the back breaking work of the past, but also opens the imagination to what this might mean in a contemporary setting. We may earn our living as a knowledge intensive economy, but battles to contain nature still exist in the present. To say 'buffer zone' with conviction and pride resonates strongly. It provokes and prompts the imagination. The mind actuates itself, it is moved to be active. Images come to mind, thoughts emerge, our fantasy is sparked up, a concept appears. The focus changes, we interrogate ourselves: 'how can you make a leftover space into a place'. Hans notes correctly: 'Things can gain significance by linking them to a modern application or spatial ambition'.

LIMES
pp 65, 66

Words matter and how you put them together as metaphors matters too as do mind pictures. Chosen well they reveal the things we sense, that is the phenomena so we can visualize them. Too often, by contrast, the language of planning and policymaking is deadening. We cannot hear or feel the meaning anymore. The lexicon includes too often the words strategy, policy, input, output, framework, sustainable development, change. They are used interchangeably and in any order.

THE THEATRE OF DIGGING
p 67

Yet to take familiar words and to put them together in a different context or order is an art. Then they can perplex, they can create consternation, but also energy and surprise. 'Digging' sounds mechanical, perfunctory, routine, dull. You simply go through the motions. Linked to the word 'theatre' 'digging' gains a new life force. It appears there is a depth and a history to digging, there is turmoil, there are highs and lows, problems occur and resolutions happen.

Wordplay is more than messing about. It is a serious business. Words strung together well bring concepts into being. They elicit insight, knowledge and set learning in motion. Not everyone is able to animate words, to generate metaphors and drag a bigger meaning out of them. It requires a certain mind. Hans has this mind.

Hans thinks artistically. For too long we thought that to be involved with these cultural processes or to think artistically you would have to be an artist. This is not the case. In fact I don't know whether Hans is an artist, what I do know is that he gives a fresh unorthodox eye to things, which is not bounded by convention. His canvas is the place he is working in and on. This can be a street, a building, a landscape or an idea. His materials rather than paints and the brush are his mental toolkit and the way he approaches questions and challenges. He is curious, so this allows him to be imaginative and with that he is able to be creative and from that inventions and innovations can emerge. These attributes foster certain qualities of mind which include: Fluidity, flexibility and feeling relaxed about ambiguity; being able to think about people and place simultaneously and so understanding the interactive relationships between the hardware and software where the physical is there to assist social relations and to enable activities to happen. There is the ability too to grasp the essence, the potential and limitations of varied disciplines from engineering, to finance, to psychology, anthropology, social activism or project management. These abilities give him the scope to think across domains, disciplines and differences.

It requires other attributes such as relaxing people, making them feel comfortable and getting them to talk. There is a need to tread a subtle path between being active, demonstrative and directive and being passive and allowing things to come to you. A fine judgement is required in assessing when to move from one mode to the next. These are interpersonal skills. In any project being alert is key: Do I push, encourage or guide? Do I link threads, summarize or do I hold back? Do I signal possibilities, provoke or foster absurd situations that get people to see new possibilities? Do I show how you turn the old into something completely new and so reveal continuity? Do I encourage divergent routes of the imagined to be explored or do I focus on the here and now? Timing and judgement is everything in assessing what is right.

Hans likes history as well as imagined futures. He is aware of the effects of simplistically erasing memory, but he knows too that it continuously needs retranslating and reinterpreting in order to revive its vitality.

BULB & BREAKFAST
pp 204-205

BULB & BREAKFAST – BLOEMENCORSO expresses this well. Time spent on cultural exploration or with history seems too long and cumbersome for many of the too rationalistic planners or developers. Yet the long term effect of helping people be who they are and to express their identity sustains places and projects and lets new cultural layers grow.

To achieve what he wants Hans needs to play some tricks. Culture and history can feel weighty, clutter the mind and make it feel too full with meaning that is desperate to get out. Superimpose on this the image warfare of the sign overloaded world of fast thinking, fast building, fast everything and the result is that many go into their shell. How, he asks, do you build in reflection in this speedy world? The freshness and clarity of an empty canvas is one answer Hans gives. His process seeks to let unmediated messages emerge that have a directness that feels true to itself. It is about 'cherishing and optimizing what exists, rather than transplanting high expectations from elsewhere'.

Opening the imagination is one thing, getting things to happen another. Here Hans throws up another counterintuitive tool from his kit: 'Playfulness'. This is reflected in his attitude where he often uses the absurd to get people to think out of their box and to look at the world differently. When you are competing with the dominant logics of planning with its cost accounting dynamics the unusual, surprise, ambiguity and the paradox often gives us the appropriate jolt. It is this that may be authentic. He also plays in a formal

THE MAKING OF
pp 94-99, 164-183

sense. By participating in his game **THE MAKING OF** you get a sense of the limitations and complexities of spatial planning in the real world. He forces the players to match their ambitions and dreams with those of others and he adds to this the phenomena and realities of the place in question. Therefore you cannot just get what you want. You make your case as part of team, you raise objections about what others want to achieve, you respond to the objections of others, you lobby and there is a jury which decides which arguments are strongest. Most importantly you understand complexity and **Hans is a manager of complexity.**

Hans calls this diversity of roles being a 'concept manager'. It is a new type of job. The method floating through his process involves project managing and co-ordinating imaginations, giving people a sense of the possible and orchestrating opinions and momentum to bring out ideas and open out things rather than closing them in as is the norm. In a sense Hans becomes a vision guardian. At the same time it involves getting things to happen.

I did not know who Hans Venhuizen was when I was asked to write a critical introduction to his book by a mutual friend. Now I wish I had met him a long time ago. I think we have a lot in common, we both wish to expand what is meant by planning. There is a desire to incorporate cultural literacy into planning, where culture is seen as a giver of insight, as a resource, a stimulator and a provocation. Too often planners treat culture as an after-thought when in fact it determines what ends up as space and place. Every type of planning has been and is cultural by definition, but we have forgotten it. People pretend there is an apparently value neutral technical approach. We want to break free from that thinking and the idea that there is a simple planning repertoire which privileges the physical and the traditional city making disciplines from quantity surveying to engineering. Drawing on what Hans writes: Culture based planning is a design process where dormant phenomena become visible so enabling them to exert an innovative influence on physical planning. It is a flexible tool, it is a perspective and a way of thinking. It is the discipline and art of making more out of planning proces-ses than the individual disciplines, components and interests could offer. It is a smarter kind of planning. Unfortunately it still does not have enough influence. I hope his book begins to change this situation.

Charles Landry is the author of *The Creative City: A Toolkit for Urban Innovators*, *The Art of City Making* and with Phil Wood *The Intercultural City: Planning for Diversity Advantage*.

SPATIAL-PLANNING

This is a book about spatial-planning culture. Spatial-planning culture is not limited to landscape design and urban design, art in the public space or the cultural history of the built environment. It is not the role played by cultural institutions in the built environment or making visible what people think of the area where they live. It is also not the efforts made by the cultural sector in the field of spatial planning, but often, something *entirely* different – or even much more. Spatial-planning culture is above all about how space is created within the time and place of a given set of actions. This book shows how the cultural power of spatial planning can be used, where unexpected qualities are lying hidden and how, with their help, connections can be made between *now* and *soon*. A prerequisite for deploying this cultural dimension of spatial planning and design is a curiosity about the widest possible range of causes leading to spatial planning as well as the consequences of such processes. In addition, enthusiasm about the situation in question, and the will critically to participate in the relevant process of change, are indispensable.

WHITE-COAT APPROACH

It was not so long ago that the spatial planning of the Netherlands was the exclusive preserve of experts in white coats working in sterile environments. Here, they tinkered primarily with the 'hardware' of the built environment, creating smart water systems, optimal infrastructure and ideal, but strictly separated, residential, work and recreation areas, this in the firm belief that such spaces would later be used to the complete satisfaction of their users. For a long time, this 'white-coat approach' worked perfectly; the world of a few decades ago was less complex and also changed less rapidly than today, and, what is more, the inhabitants of this country did not find it very urgent to start involving themselves intensively in the planning of their (residential) environments. This all changed in the 1970s, when continuing protests against the further realization of functional spatial plans in the form, amongst other things, of new motorways, airports and extensive

CULTURE

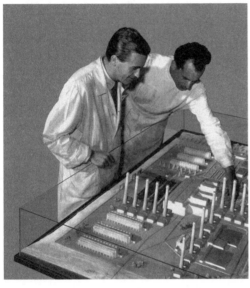

Spatial planning in white coats.

urban expansion, could no longer be defused. Ultimately, this opened the door to far-reaching changes in the planning process, in which, as a rule, the public had not been welcome.

Even at the lowest level of scale, spatial planning involves a complex interplay of interconnected needs and interests. Even in one's own living room, user-requirements must be facilitated within both the space available and the constraints of one's financial possibilities, whilst at the same time taking account of one's aesthetic criteria. Or, put in another way: the furniture, which has been selected in accordance with one's tastes and pocket-book, has to be arranged in such a way that it can be used to its full potential and, in addition, in such a way that it is visually pleasing. When it comes to furnishing one's own living room, the number of individuals involved can easily be kept track of, and the available possibilities have often already been pre-shaped by the architect. Choices that have turned out less successful than others can always be undone without difficulty. However, the higher the level of scale of the spatial planning process involved, the greater the complexity of its component factors; the number of parties, relevant interests and requisite financial resources increases, whilst the possibility of undoing poor choices decreases proportionately. At the level of scale where spatial planning actually takes place, the possibilities for trying things are very few indeed.

ILLUSTRATION MAKERS

Ten years ago, it was still passionately argued that the white-coat approach, also referred to as 'top-down planning', should entirely be replaced by bottom-up processes. Since then, this standpoint has been succeeded by a broad spectrum of hybrid processes, and I rarely hear someone still calling for the exclusive use of the bottom-up approach. Whilst in small-scale projects involving the (re-)planning of the immediate residential environment the challenge of including the many interests and interested parties in a worthwhile process is substantial enough, with a planning process at the highest level of scale, and at that, intended to reach deep into the future, the challenge is well-nigh impossible.

In the search for possibilities to put flesh on that impalpable future, an increasingly prominent place is being assigned to design and designers; after all, ours is a pictorial culture in which seeing *is* believing. By placing the emphasis on the end-picture, the process of underlying choices, principles and ideas disappears from view, whilst it is in these very things that the fuel is to be found for insight into the measures and special twists involved in the development process. In such processes, the presentation of an end-picture quickly leads to a paradoxically calming effect, since the end-picture is the last thing that we can predict. Rather than defining measures that bring into focus the prerequisites for the desired development but leave open the end-picture itself, the design-based investigation shifts the focus to determining the prerequisites for the purpose of arriving at the desired end-picture.

MONEY SHOTS

At the present moment, we are experiencing the high-water mark of a trend whereby, at all levels of scale in the spatial planning process, a seductive perspective, packaged in an attractive end-picture, is deployed in order to generate the requisite dynamic, excitement and, thus, support base for the changes in question. Many of these pictures are, however, mendacious in nature. Referred to as 'money shots' in the film world, such end-pictures are used essentially as everything-is-going-to-be-okay inebriants, intended to becloud the actual situation. The chances of the beckoning end-picture ever becoming reality are as small as the disappointment it will cause will be great. What generates the most energetic support base and most concerted dynamic is wide-ranging insight into the underlying choices, principles and ideas of the plan in question, accompanied by curiosity about the spatial effects these ultimately will bring. For many municipal administrators who have come to realize that their village or city is increasingly (becoming) the subject of competition, this is a far too uncertain path. And so, they continue to try to attract investors, new residents and companies with a stunning presentation of a fantasized shining future.

INSPIRATION

When presenting their proposals and ideas, designers, as well as politicians, often deploy works of art as a way of illustrating the source from which they derive their inspiration. When someone explains his/her decision, design or vision on the basis of being 'inspired' by one source or another, extra vigilance is, however, in order. Invoking such a source of inspiration generally conjures up an attractive and highly appealing 'zone' where the ideas of the designer or politician in question appear to have gained a foothold. It is not exceptional for inspiration to be trotted out as something having a positive influence on the achievement being presented, whilst, on closer inspection, that influence is nowhere to be found. One is therefore well-advised, in connection with a 'claim of inspiration', to check whether the inspiring examples in question are not just being deployed as crowd-pleasers or lubricants, and thus, as a camouflage for a lacking mastery of the concept.

Observation, 2003

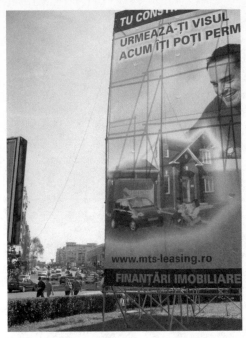

The perfect home in Bucharest.

Rather than trying to dazzle one's audience with seductive perspectives to hide one's uncertainty about the future, this *Manual
for Cultural Spatial Planning* demonstrates how, on the contrary,
by assiduously pursuing an uncertain path it is possible to profit
greatly from every situation in which change is being undergone.
The greatest task thus lies not in drowning out insecurity, but
rather, in welcoming it and translating it into curiosity: a curiosity
which slowly but surely will lead to a wide-ranging insight into
the situation undergoing change, and will in any case ultimately
be the most productive option in terms of the support base, identity and particularization of the situation.

 The handbook begins with a treatment of the effects of
end-pictures and the unique and productive outcomes that are
prevented through a stubborn belief in the use of such pictures.
In turn, I discuss the process of designing the *uncertain path* and
the importance of equipping the process with a strong identity.
The three chapters which follow reveal how a process of change
can lead to more identity and individuality of character: by recog-
nising the value of the history, as well as the built-in limitations,
of the landscape in question, and by using the actual relevant
culture, rather than one that is wished for. Finally, I show how
such 'found qualities' can indeed play a role in the process of
change. The book shows how one can translate the most divergent of qualities into robust processes of change through the use
of a game matrix and a well-designed process, and by involving
a concept manager. In analysing situations undergoing change
as well as actually driving processes of change, the relationship
between play and seriousness occupies a prominent place. This
handbook shows how, by using the principle of play in a variety
of incarnations, one opens the door to a more cultural kind of
spatial planning, which I have dubbed Game Urbanism.

ALLES WIRD

In the battle for a prosperous future being fought by cities and regions, fascinating projects are being developed under the headings *place branding* and *city branding*. The cities and regions – but urban districts, neighbourhoods and tiny villages as well – that take part, are defined as 'brands' with the potential to create distinct profiles for themselves on the urban-competition market. Out of a fear to miss the boat to the future, branding firms are engaged, debate evenings organized, scenarios drafted and campaigns launched. Typically, at the start of such processes, an attempt is made to obtain unity amongst all the interested parties, including administrators, the business sector and residents, to ensure that everyone can identify with the brand to be developed. This early effort to obtain unity has two consequences: the specific character of one's own environment is robbed of its uniqueness, and a tendency develops to fixate on the positive qualities being wished for at that moment in time. As a result, the special opportunities waiting to be discovered are overlooked.

SINCERE AND AUTHENTIC STAGINGS

The practice on the part of cities of doing their best to disseminate an optimal image of themselves in the outside world, is not something that was first invented in this century. The second half of the 1950s witnessed a veritable deluge of books for the purpose of 'city marketing' before such a term existed. Cities and towns all over Europe engaged photographers to prove how their location had overcome the ravages of the Second World War and was now on the road to a shining future. As the moments with the desired message were often difficult to capture, many of the photos were staged, for example the cleanly outfitted young man who, in post-war Berlin, mounts a scaffolding without the slightest hint of being a construction worker, or the woman dressed in the height of fashion who makes living in industrialized residential housing suddenly seem so attractive. What make these photos so authentic is the extremely 'sincere' manner of their staging. Without exception, all of the photo books present the

GUT

The perfect builder in about 1955.

same picture: a city with both a history *and* a future, with both old *and* new, a city for shopping, working, study and residence, with culture, nature, relaxation and, above all, people.

INTERCHANGEABLE IDIOSYNCRASY

The urban look to be found in these publications from the 1950s is in perfect harmony with how present-day municipal administrators want to be seen. And even if they are preceded by a broad-based public process, the typologies of urban identity employed are invariably the same. They are often turned into 'exciting' slogans, which, when placed side-by-side, offer a valuable look into self-insight: cities are *up to it* like Almere, *exciting* like Roermond or *daring* like Rotterdam. Alliterations emphasize that these cities have *essences*: they offer jobs and enjoyment, build and bind or are congenial, like the country. They take things

The perfect town in about 1959.

AMUSEMENT-PARKIZATION

In the course of time, cities and villages have been indelibly marked by a process of grappling with the limitations presented by the technologies available and the materials present. Local traditions and region-specific architectural styles came about as a natural product of this process. All such technical limitations have now triumphantly been overcome: in the construction field, virtually anything can now be built anywhere. Local traditions are making place for global habits. It is only economic factors that still occasionally throw a spanner in the works and impose limitations. How can a building, a square or a city still distinguish itself? Actually, the only things that still count are image and entertainment value: buildings and cities sell themselves by means of unusual exteriors or an ability to provide amusement. The city of blood, sweat and tears has turned into a flashy trademark – a 'logo'. The world is being turned into an amusement park, conceived in terms of urban-planning and architectural scenarios, filled to the brim with buildings as stage props and designed as a thematic experience. Copying and simulation are accepted as original and legitimate practices.

Perception, 1995

in hand, enjoy to the full and are enterprising in natural surroundings. They are many-facetted, make more things possible and are, in addition, more than just beautiful. They characterize themselves as *original* and *authentic,* with both *urban allure* and *rural charm*. And what comes of all this many-facettedness? A high degree of interchangeability. Regardless whether the city in question is located beside a Norwegian fjord, on the German-Polish border, on a slushy Dutch peat bog or on the east coast of China: all of the prospectuses display the same wished-for urbanity before the backdrop of a geographical and cultural reality which functions merely as a decor.

With all of this city marketing, cities frequently fail to notice the most distinctive of their qualities, the ones which represent the greatest challenges and which tend to be viewed in a negative light. For example, the city of Den Helder, Noord-Holland, (pop. > 50,000) thinks that with the slogan 'A special city with a special location' and an investment in its somewhat seedy shopping street, it will even be able to attract tourists away from the nearby holiday island, Texel. This, whilst its real opportunities lie in two developments that are generally viewed negatively. Firstly, Den Helder is experiencing a decrease in population due to a disappearance of employment opportunities and to the associated urban shrinkage, which is become increasingly noticeable. With the motto 'Den Helder: more space every day', the city would present itself in a much more honest manner and be in a better position to make the most of its opportunities. Secondly, it could actually take advantage of the generally unwelcomed summer traffic jams created by holiday makers heading for the ferry to Texel, rather than trying to eliminate them, as is now planned, either by means of a bridge or tunnel or even by relocating the entire ferry harbour. This, whilst, just like at airports, such sojourns could be viewed as an excellent commercial opportunity. A system of guaranteed time slots could be developed for those driving to the ferry. Whilst this might result in slightly longer waiting times, it would eliminate the need to plod along in one's car at 2 km/hr. One could park the car at the old naval harbour, go shopping or visit a restaurant or museum, thus enjoying the waiting time, getting to know Den Helder and leaving some money behind.

URBAN THERAPY

Cities that tinker extensively with their image/personality or even call in city-branding specialists to administer 'urban therapy', bear many similarities to the participants in make-over programmes on television – those extremely run-of-the-mill people who, for decades, have felt tormented by poor teeth, a deformed chin or other aesthetic problem and, as a result, have entirely given up doing anything at all about their appearance. They feel imprisoned in an aesthetic isolation, and, consequently, have had their self-confidence reduced to an absolute minimum, which generally has had a negative effect on the quality of their friendships and careers. Fortunately, the make-over programmes have come to their aid in arranging a great turnaround – read: metamorphosis – in their fortunes, which in turn is shown, as a source of inspiration, to a wide audience. However, once they have shot the programmes for television, their producers never pay a return visit to the subjects of the shows, to see what has remained of their new élan, but rather, dive energetically into a new success story in the making.

Urban renewal projects take a similar course. A feeling of isolation is often remedied by exclusively aesthetic means. The greatest difference, however, lies in the incommensurability of the work-intensiveness required for changing a city, as opposed to an individual. A city can be provided with a new 'mug' quite quickly – with flags and fountains, but every intervention in the hardware of a city calls for long-term research, design and decision-making processes. The spectrum involved is too great to be presented in appealing and quickly concocted 'before' and 'after' shots.

SPECTACULAR SHRINKAGE

In situations featuring city branding and other forms of 'planism' there is inherently a strained relationship between how the status quo and the wished-for future perspective are analysed and presented. Some municipalities explain the need for a wished-for change by presenting the current situation as problematic. *If the need for an intervention is so clear, the public will perhaps not be so critical about the nature and extent of the changes* is how the municipality's thinking goes in such cases. Prior to German reunification, the part of the GDR which is now the state of Sachsen-Anhalt, was, due to a large number of chemical factories and associated industrial activity, more healthy economically

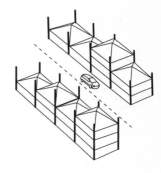

HOUSING STACK

Increasingly, people can be said to have 'residential careers': in each phase of life, they live in a different home, according to what is most appropriate for that phase, and thus regularly exchange their old living environment for a new one. Each change in one's household situation prompts a move to a new home, which also means leaving a residential environment which, in many cases, has only gradually and with great effort become one's own. The sustainability of the residential environment today so widely aspired to is not only a question of the materials used to build it, but depends, above all, on continuity of residence, and the continuance of the involvement of residents with their environment. The housing stack, the residential variant of the haystack, makes it possible to modify one's home in accordance with each phase of life and household situation without this leading to an increase in one's spatial consumption. Extra floors can be built in connection with marriages, births, the moving-in of invalid parents or starting a business in one's own home. Floors can then be removed in connection with divorce, the children's leaving home, death of the invalid parent(s) or bankruptcy. The floors, built using a standard prefab-system, can in turn be sold on to other housing-stack residents who are expanding their homes. As a result of this process, the roof landscape of the housing-stack district will regularly change in appearance.

Proposal in connection with the project
UNDERCOVER, Arnhem, 1997

49

URBAN GLUTAMATE

Sometimes, the menus of Chinese restaurants indicate not only whether traces of nuts are to be found in the dishes on offer, or that preservatives are used in their preparation, but, in addition, whether monosodium glutamate has been added to them. The most important property of monosodium glutamate is its intensification of the typical flavour characteristics of foods, whilst itself having neither flavour nor colour. To put it more precisely, adding monosodium glutamate to food actually does not intensify its taste, but rather, makes one more sensitive to that taste, functioning, if you like, as a lubricant for the taste buds, and thus stimulating our desire to eat. In this way, monosodium glutamate plays an intermediary role between food and eater, causing the latter to value the food in question more highly because it seems to be fuller and more intense in flavour. Just as in its cuisine, monosodium glutamate is also liberally used in China's cities. In other words, additives are used in order to make buildings and/or their function more easily palatable. Obvious examples of this practice are the propaganda slogans that pop up everywhere, both in the cities and on billboards along the motorways. Their edifying sentiments, such as *Let us create the most civilized district in the province* or *Architecture embraces nature. Life becomes art*, are almost always before a background of attractive urban skylines. For this type of propaganda, the classic red background has virtually disappeared; here, the city itself is the lubricant which is targeted at the postcommunist Chinese citizen.

Perception, Xiamen, China, 2006

speaking than it was as a living environment. Only a very small portion of these industrial estates survived the *Wende*, and only a fraction of the original jobs have remained. As Sachsen-Anhalt has been unsuccessful in positioning itself sufficiently strongly on the battlefield of European regions, it has undergone a spectacular reduction in its population and a proportionate increase in unoccupied housing. This situation prompted Bauhaus Dessau to initiate an *Internationale Bauausstellung* (IBA) with, as its theme, the phenomenon of urban shrinkage.

One of the IBA projects took place in the spring of 2004 in a small city to the south of Magdeburg, Stassfurt, whose population has, in recent years, decreased by twenty percent to about 20,000. Whereas prior to reunification, the industrial activity around Stassfurt was directly or indirectly connected with the potassium mines that lie beneath it, these have now all been closed and industrial activity has largely disappeared. Despite years of positive expectations and optimistic planning, it has not been possible to provide new, sustainable employment opportunities for the citizens of Stassfurt and, thus, to bind them to the city and its environs. They continue to move away, whilst the homes they leave vacant do not attract new residents. Not only are the *Plattenbau* districts – the areas dominated by prefab concrete residential housing largely intended for the city's labourers – becoming deserted, but the historic city centre is also plagued by decline.

This has prompted the creation of a *Rückbau* or 'regressive building' programme, which provides for planned urban shrinkage in order to absorb the consequences of the mass exodus of the city's population. In this case, however, *Rückbau* is actually a euphemism for demolition, which has become unavoidable due to poor economic prospects. But, as demolition does not sell well, many municipal administrators have chosen, against their better judgement, to continue to make *alles-wird-gut* (everything-is-going-to-be-okay) predictions, based on purely speculative assumptions – the necessary step backward is presented as a leap forward.

ARTIST'S-IMPRESSION-ISM

In Stassfurt, twelve teams of architects, landscape architects and urban planners who live and/or work in Sachsen-Anhalt were brought together for the IBA project. The core question is: what can be done to help the historic city centre once again to play a prominent role in the life of the city? All of the proposals submitted are imbued with the *alles-wird-gut* approach, the unshakeable belief that, if an investor can be attracted, this will make possible the completion of the planning process, appropriately accompanied by an artist's-impression-ist presentation. The designers propose to rebuild the historic structure of the city centre, heavily damaged by mine collapses, with newbuild, in which, in reality, no investor or prospective tenant will be interested.

The city's administrators, who, in contrast to the designers, actually have insight into the present urban dynamic, are decidedly disappointed with this outcome. They resolve not to opt for the designers' *alles-wird-gut* end-pictures. Spurred on by a public planning process, they pull the plug on the costly pumping plant that keeps the imploded portion of the city centre dry, allowing a unique inner-city lake to form. They give up the quest for what they wanted to have, and embrace what they have; in doing so, they are extraordinarily authentic.

'A city is never finished' is an often-heard cliché. Nevertheless, many urban administrators and planners regularly do their best to convince the public that the completion of their city is around the corner, or that they are, in any case, particularly well-positioned with regard to doing so. Like men in a midlife crisis, such cities encourage fast sport cars to drive through their streets; they dress excessively casually, appear at festivals that are too hip for their age and wear themselves thin with new hobbies, such as competitions for the greenest municipality, nicest city centre or best city-marketing slogan; they dream of attaining the status of European Capital of Culture or even becoming the site of the Olympics. The *alles-wird-gut* approach is deeply rooted in the genes of urban administrators.

A DYNAMIC

With many people, change primarily elicits a reaction of fear, and, as spatial planning inherently involves several parties, there are at least as many fears to be allayed in a given planning process as there are parties. Implementing changes calls for wide and active support, a dynamic, and movement. The fears about the changes must convincingly be taken away or, in any case, sufficiently compensated for, or, at least, neutralized. The first design involved in a process of change, even before the first proposals are made, is that of the identity of the process. A well-formulated process identity, can, by identifying the positive qualities of a location in the right optimistic tone, generate much involvement and, in turn, the required dynamic amongst the interested parties. Nothing moves without a dynamic. However, an end-picture that is based on a lie will generate the wrong dynamic, which will in turn have a negative effect on the process of change.

DES BEEMSTERS

When, in 1999, UNESCO granted world-heritage status to the Beemster, the initial joy and pride of some inhabitants of the polder quickly changed to concern. They wondered what this actually meant in concrete terms. Would the entire polder become a museum? Would it then be put under lock and key, so that agricultural exploitation of this highly fertile part of Holland would no longer be possible? Experts were able to explain that the Beemster's qualities "deserved the highest degree of protection," but were unable precisely to indicate what this protection meant for this economically thriving polder. Following various inventories and assessments aimed at identifying and inventorying these qualities, the situation gained in urgency through a protest action by the environmental organization, Milieufederatie Noord-Holland, against the enlargement of the cheese factory located in the polder, as well as Milieufederatie's establishment, together with the Municipality of Beemster and the Province of Noord-Holland, of a working group for the purpose of clearly identifying the polder's (cultural heritage) qualities. In 2005,

WITHOUT LIES

DES BEEMSTERS logo. Design: Studio Minke Themans

the question as to the significance of the polder's world heritage status in the context of current spatial planning found its way to an ad-hoc combination consisting of Bureau Venhuizen, Steenhuis stedenbouw/landschap, and Redscape Landscape and Urbanism. The investigations, interviews and debate/game sessions in the context of **THE MAKING OF**, as well as the relevant case studies which followed, resulted in the development vision, **DES BEEMSTERS**. This vision in turn grew into a comprehensive approach for actively and successfully involving (cultural-heritage) qualities in the discussion of current spatial-planning issues concerning the polder.

The *concept*, 'Des Beemsters', was actually the first portion to be realized within this development vision. 'Des Beemsters' is a way of expressing in words, and with the greatest possible brevity, what is intrinsic in the situation at hand. **DES BEEMSTERS** provides the Beemster a 'brand name' to the process of adjusting the polder to current developments, a brand name that is not connected to a specific sector, but rather to what is intrinsic to

DES BEEMSTERS water table, 2008.

SQUAREABOUTS

Although it was in part because of the Beemster's grid of dead-straight roads, with crossings at right angles, that UNESCO granted it world-heritage status, it is precisely this pattern that makes driving in the polder so hazardous. At various dangerous crossings, roundabouts of a type entirely foreign to this world heritage site pop up, and not in the middle of the crossings, but just to the side. The roads branch off a short distance before the crossing – a modification that has resulted in a substantial worsening of the original situation. Naturally, this was not done maliciously, but rather, because it appeared to be "the only possible solution." In point of fact, the best solution to the problem is to be found in the polder's original plan, in which square-shaped squares are indicated at all crossings. These squares were never realized. By realising them now, the resulting 'squareabouts' would lead to a significant improvement in the traffic situation, whilst leaving all relevant qualities intact. What's more: through the solving of a current problem, the Beemster would become more itself than ever.

Perception/proposal in the context of **DES BEEMSTERS**, 2005

the entire polder. As a result, Des Beemsters allows cultural heritage to form an integral part of the current culture of the polder and the spatial planning processes pertaining to it, and in turn, to become more than just another item on the ever-longer spatial planning checklist.

The development vision, **DES BEEMSTERS**, does not, indeed, provide a reassuring document in the form of a 'cultural-heritage value map' on which the precise locations of the various values constituting this world heritage site are highlighted in different colours, so that they in turn can be protected. **DES BEEMSTERS** declares the entire polder, from its ring dike up to and including its farms and their houses, cultural heritage, and identifies and inventories how the relevant values have come into being. The special rules governing this process are, to a far greater extent than the existing situation/monuments, what actually constitutes this world heritage site. And it is entirely feasible to translate these rules into the spatial-planning tasks of the present moment. The results of such a translation may not bear any resemblance to the results obtained in the past, but they do provide a guarantee for culture-historical continuity.

In 2007, the Des Beemsters development vision was translated into nineteen projects, as well as the founding of Bureau Des Beemsters. Bureau Des Beemsters is the point within the Municipality of Beemster where the projects' various facets, e.g., spatial guidelines, culture-historical knowledge and expertise, process design and communication, converge. The desired 'highest possible degree of protection' for the Beemster is assembled, from its constituent parts, under the supervision of this bureau. Three projects, which were completed in 2009, are in the process of being directly anchored in the new development plan for the polder's outlying areas. The different paths of enquiry forming the focal points of the **DES BEEMSTERS** projects bear a resemblance to ones being pursued in other rural areas in the Netherlands, but are distinguished from them by their **DES BEEMSTERS** approach. Bureau Des Beemsters will cease to exist in 2012, when the polder will have existed for exactly 400 years, and at which time the spatial updating of the polder for the present generation will

56

GASTGASTGEBER Oberhausen, with KITEV.
Image editing by Bureau Venhuizen

🏠 **bulb&breakfast**

BULB & BREAKFAST

The Dutch Bulb Region is a landscape that is dominated by the pursuit of ever-greater industrialization of the process of flower bulb production. In the past, this production, and consequently, the land-scape, was dominated by special bulb sheds, which owed their construction to the limited possibilities existing at the time for the climate-controlled conditions required for storing flower bulbs. Today, the climate can be controlled to a much higher standard in halls equipped with cooling systems, and as a result, many a bulb shed has become obsolete. It is easy for the owners of such historic sheds to obtain a demolition permit for them. Ironically, this policy was instituted in the interests of spatial quality, as a way to prevent the attraction to these areas of carpet showrooms and other forms of re-use, along with their undesirable side effects. By means of the competi-tion, **BULB & BREAKFAST**, possibilities were identified and inventoried for responsible, meaningful re-use of this cultural herit-age, without the need to alter the objects very much, namely, by realising season-linked, and thus temporary, lodging facil-ities in the sheds. The **BULB & BREAKFAST** formula thus appears to fit perfectly into the broader category of 'cultural-heritage lodgings.' Ideas are also currently being sought for the re-use of brick factories (Brick & Breakfast), bunker complexes (Bomb & Breakfast) and old farmhouses (Barn & Breakfast).

Competition/project in the context of
SOUL AND SOIL, 2002–2004
Image based on the results
of the prize winners.

have been brought to completion. If all goes according to plan, the concept, Des Beemsters, will disappear in parallel to the Bureau's disbanding (see further pp 136-151).

GASTGASTGEBER

Process identity is of essential importance where the goal is to cajole the most divergent of parties, each of which prefers to work as autonomously as possible, into participating together in a process. This involves more than just formulating a common end-objective, although even this can be extremely problematic, as each interested party will have a different end-objective in mind. In such cases, it is best to seek a connection amongst the parties that lies outside the context of their divergent concrete objectives. In this regard, a unifying, practical task can lead to the formation of a collective organization, which from this basis, can in turn gradually take on more and more concrete signifi-cance within the whole.

In 2010, the German *Ruhrgebiet*, will, together with the cities, Istanbul and Pécs, be a European capital of culture. Numerous Dutch cultural organizations and individual artists, and several Dutch cities, as well, have taken the initiative to develop projects and activities in the context of RUHR.2010, in many cases in cooperation with German partners. In early 2009, Lucas Verweij, Boris Sieverts and I were commissioned by the Dutch govern-ment to devise a unifying theme for the more than 100 initiatives (from the widest possible variety of culture initiators) now in progress. It quickly became clear that we would not be able to give form to this unifying theme in content terms; most of the cultural initiators had already for some time been developing their projects in cooperation with their partners, and had already formulated both approaches and themes. There was no longer room for someone playing the classical directorial role, formu-lating the content at the beginning of the creative process, and

GASTGASTGEBER Oberhausen
by Studio Makkink & Bey. Photo: Eric Dil

BEACONS

With the project, **SPACE FOR BEACONS**, possibilities have been identified for erecting new beacons along the River Waal, which in or around 2010 is set to undergo a large-scale facelift. The only beacons along the river that are actually referred to as beacons are the traffic signs that indicate the location of the fairway to captains. The other beacons along the river with which people are familiar, e.g., chimneys, bridges and church towers, were never intended purely as beacons in the landscape, but rather, were each erected for a different specific function. As a result of their clear presence extending over longer periods of time, these structures have come to have much more meaning than originally intended, and have thus taken on the status of beacons. It is important that this process also be respected with regard to the new beacons yet to come. Within the context of **SPACE FOR BEACONS**, the new beacons will not be created by placing the largest possible autonomous works of art along the river. By involving artists, architects and designers in the scheduled processes of change, (dike shifting, renaturation, recreation, as well as building on river forelands), such situations have the potential rapidly to develop into the beacons of the future. The possibilities for this can be found in both likely, and unlikely, situations. Further, it should be noted that beacons do not develop exclusively from 'nice' points of departure – new beacons can also have their basis in the problematics of dredging or the designing of new industrial parks.

Plan for the project, **SPACE FOR BEACONS**, Province of Gelderland, 2009

thus giving direction to the overall development process. What's more, most of the cultural institutions involved operated on as autonomous a basis as possible from within their individual disciplines, with their own objectives, and indeed benefited from the opportunity to present their own distinct individuality to as high a degree as possible. It ultimately became clear that if there was a connection to be made between the various projects, it could never have been found in their content, but rather, the practical side of the situation.

The Ruhrgebiet is roughly 30 by 80 km in size, and has a number of urban nuclei – it is thus not the case that there is only one place where a great tower can be built to advertise one's presence here. To get to know the region, it is advisable to reserve several days for the purpose. Anyone expecting an abundance of exciting places to lodge will, however, be disappointed, as we found. Further, for the capital-of-culture year itself, all hotels appear to have been booked solid, far in advance, for fairs and other events, so that any visitors/participants seeking lodging must do this far removed from the Ruhrgebiet itself. It was this very situation that inspired **GASTGASTGEBER** (German for Guest Host). **GASTGASTGEBER** is essentially a Netherlands-based project for creating temporary, interesting and mobile hotel facilities for the duration of the RUHR.2010 capital-of-culture year, for those attending the event and its projects. The timings and locations of these hotel facilities are linked to concentrations of Dutch cultural presentations, but are also in and of themselves centres for design and pictorial art. In this way, the Netherlands, whilst a guest in the Ruhrgebiet, can at the same time act as host.

Through its role as a 'connector', **GASTGASTGEBER** will be able to link up with the widest possible range of culture initiators, as well as to convince a number of hesitant parties to develop projects for Ruhr.2010. The lodging facilities are being designed by Dutch designers. **GASTGASTGEBER** is not a tower visible from every corner of the Ruhrgebiet, but a network that stimulates movement, and attracts activities, across the entire area.

The greatest single impediment to process identities is that they anticipate desired end-results to an excessive degree, and, as result, risk propagating what is actually a dishonest end-picture. An end-picture can, in fact, only be arrived at based on numerous speculations and with the help of several interpretations that can never exclusively be based on an objectively verifiable, expected result. A largely speculative character in turn feeds the distrust that is present, and thus stands in the way of a successful process of change. A successful process identity takes the process of change itself as its point of departure. By not starting out with an end-picture, but rather, by basing itself on the qualities of the search process, it stimulates involvement, curiosity, familiarity and excitement and, thus, a dynamic. Process identities are the pioneers of change; they pave the way and make change liveable. Process identities are not the property of one of the interested parties, but rather, that of the process of change itself. Process identities are, indeed, by definition, temporary. If they have been successful, they are surpassed by their results, and in this way, quickly, and as a matter of course, consigned to oblivion.

SOCIETY FOR THE PRESERVATION OF THE MCDONALD'S POLE

Much of what now surrounds us is destined, at some point in time, to become cultural heritage, but just like the Dutch farmer who interwove his Maasheggen (now considered historically valuable), or the engineer who designed his Dutch water line (now recognized as a monument), we do not yet regard the items we now create as cultural heritage. And that is indeed fortunate, since this would likely make nervous wrecks of us. For some things, however, it is important to make an exception. The McDonald's pole, the most significant beacon in the built environment from the last fifteen years, is such an exception. Even if someone is an inveterate vegetarian, a practicing Hindu or a hater of junk food, the yellow M on this high pole has indelibly been etched into his/her consciousness. The yellow M is a beacon for motorway users, be they hamburger eaters or not. By being so eminently visible and dividing our route into bite-sized portions, it is a source of support to the motorway user: a McDonald's is never far away. Yellow was originally used for the company's 'golden arches', but it has proved highly useful as a universal colour trademark for the company as it is easy to reproduce and contrasts strongly with sky blue. When, in the not-too-distant future, the economic tide starts turning for this hamburger giant, it is imperative that this piece of future cultural heritage be preserved for posterity – so that for years to come, we will continue to be able to divide or journeys into bite-sized portions.

Proposal, 2010

To be sure, cultural history is a legitimate field of scientific enquiry. However, when it comes to promoting the continuity of culture-historical qualities in the built environment, scientists should preferably be kept at a critical distance. Scientists are usually highly knowledgeable with regard to such subjects as the landscape and its use in the past, but in indicating its value, they are primarily interested in telling us what this value was in the past, whereas promoting the continuity of such qualities calls for transformation and interpretation, with the aim of generating value for the present day. It calls for making connections between historical qualities and current ambitions, and, to accomplish this, requires a different kind of thoroughness than the scientific kind. Rather than just looking at the expression of cultural heritage in the built environment, we must focus our attention on how this expression came about and can continue to come about. It is not enough just to regard 'things' as authentic; above all, we must regard as authentic the very manner in which they came about within the constraints of the time(s) in question, such as location, technology and political considerations. And just as important, if not even more important, than preserving the things we regard as authentic, is the imperative to be authentic with respect to the culture of our actions in the present day.

SORRY

The aborigines had had to wait 200 years for it, but in 2008, the time had finally come. On Australia's national holiday, Australia Day, the progressive prime minister, Kevin Rudd, announced that he was proud of the culture of the aborigines. On behalf of the Australian government, he did something that all his predecessors had refused to do: he said SORRY for two centuries of systematic oppression and forced westernization of the original inhabitants of the country. For many years, Australia's history was written from the perspective of the 'victors', in other words the conquerors, and the nation praised the English deportees who heroically had brought civilization to this inhospitable land.

WHAT YOU WANT IT TO BE

It honoured the industrious pioneers who had given their lives
so that the country could be built, and who, in a gradual process, had also taken the 'requisite' lives of those to whom the
country had originally belonged, the aborigines, or indigenous
Australians. From the perspective of today's predilection for
authenticity, the designation 'indigenous Australians' already
actually contains an admission of guilt, and thus an admission
that the oppression of this culture did take place.

Today's victors appear not to behave like classic victors. In
place of a widespread, blatant pride about their historic achieve-
ments, they exhibit a clear awareness of the misdeeds of their
forebears, upon which their present power is based. Critical ex-
aminations of colonialism and the slave trade also form a normal
part of today's history books. It can, indeed, do no harm – after
all, there is no danger that, through such actions, what has been
achieved could ever be lost. In addition, such historical insight
underscores above all the notion that today's Australia is open
and just, with equal opportunities for everyone.

MAROCCANON

History is never objective, but rather, is, by definition, written
based on a subjective, present-day perspective. Aside from its
scientific function, history appears primarily to be used as a tool
for shaping public opinion. For example, there are reasons to
have serious doubts about the recent boom in projects involving
history and culture-historical awareness as reflected in the built
environment. Such projects are, to be sure, idealistically motivat-
ed, but they nevertheless fall under the aegis of a generation of
indigenous white men at the end of their active careers. They are
well aware that the multicultural society will not go away quietly,
and that it will also not supplely transition back into the familiar,
trusted post-Cold War, with only slight, exclusively welcome
modifications. Within a few years, 50% of the population of the
large Dutch cities will consist of people whose parents were not
born in the Netherlands. What will they regard as their history?
Besides the Historical Canon of the Netherlands, perhaps there
will soon appear a Maroccanon, or the history of the Netherlands

as viewed from the perspective of immigrants. Not all cultural and political opinion-shapers of the present moment would welcome such diversity and source-change with open arms. And the efforts currently being made once and for all to determine the history and distinguishing culture-historical features of the Netherlands, can indeed also be seen in this light.

WAR THEME PARK

If one looks at the marks history has left on our landscapes and cities, it is ultimately those that have resulted from acts of war that emerge as the deepest. Every year, remembrances take place for the Second World War; the time is not yet right for ending this tradition. A question that *is* regularly posed, is: what should be done with our military heritage, with the 'guilty landscapes', with our memories of war and violence?

In the context of the remembrance ceremonies held in September 2007 for the (from the standpoint of the Allies) entirely unsuccessful Battle of Arnhem in 1944, artistHans Jungerius built a replica of a German bunker. Inside the bunker, visitors the could play violent war games on a computer, and the newest version of the game *Medal of Honour*, was presented, with the battle of Arnhem as its 'game-board'. With these features, Jungerius struck a nerve within the remembrance culture. Second World War remembrance ceremonies still recall the heroes and victims from 1940–1945, but hardly offer any support with regard to the young people of today who are confronted with violence. A location is needed where a connection can be made between historical and current manifestations of violence. After all, violence forms part of human nature, and in world history, peace forms the exception rather than the rule.

In the context of remembering the failed Battle of Arnhem, I put together, in the early 1990s, the **TANKRAD** (Tankwheel) as a symbol for a violence theme park. The aim of the A Bridge too Far theme park was to make it possible actively to connect current

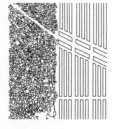

POTSDAM

The architecture of the German city of Potsdam, which borders on Berlin, is characterized by a collection of architectural styles borrowed from buildings and park designs in other cities. The city's history, too, strongly reflects the contributions of Frenchmen, Dutchmen and Russians, who, at some point in the past, had reasons to be in the city where the German Kaiser spent his summers. In the eighteenth century, for example, Dutchmen helped improve the city's water management and were, for this purpose, lodged in the still extant Dutch Quarter. At the present time, such foreigners no longer have a reason to build in Potsdam, but this tradition could be continued by those, who by virtue of their origin, do have such reasons: e.g., Vietnamese, Africans and Eastern Europeans, who at the present time comprise the typical mix of immigrants found in Potsdam, and who, as a result, would also be able to leave the stamp of their architectural traditions on the city. And the sharply contrasting adjacent Turkish, Vietnamese and Russian districts thus realized would have nothing in common with ghettoization, but rather, promote the growth of mutual respect.

Observation/proposal in the context of Eutopia, Potsdam, 1995

64

SAUSAGE FROM THE BATTLEFIELD

violent impulses – both societal and individual – as well as our experiences with violence, with the grim warnings communicated by the horrors of the past. The visitor is actually able to enter into a situation in which his/her life is at risk. The memory of the Second World War is linked to the park's attractions and the general manner in which the park functions. Because the horrors of the past are becoming more and more difficult to present in a credible manner, the theme park avoids an all too romantic approach to the past, and makes it possible for violent experiences to be undergone and felt in a direct manner. As of 2010, the park has still not been realized, and remembering violence, and experiencing it, continue to be two separate worlds.

THE FUTURE OF HISTORY

Generally speaking, objects that have culture-historical meaning are less dominant and indestructible than military bunkers. By definition, the discussion concerning the use and representation of cultural heritage in the built environment moves between two extremes. On the one hand, the view of both professional and amateur cultural historians who, with all appropriate reservations, and many lacunae and interpretations, connect the historical fragments found at a given site to form an apparently coherent narrative. On the other, the spatial consumer, who prefers to see history 'brought to life' in an appealing manner: i.e., as a myth. In other words: the world of rotting Roman pole stumps in the ground, accompanied by meticulous explanations, versus making a hole in a depiction of the world of Asterix and Obelix on a plate, and placing it around your head. But it is not a matter of opting for one of these extremes. There are so many ways to approach cultural heritage. What is required of us is, in each given situation, to choose a position between these two extremes, or to combine them.

A case in point: Romans and Batavi once walked where there is now a landscape park between Arnhem and Nijmegen, but failed to leave buildings or other artefacts behind, which could now be restored or reconstructed. The fact that 2000 years ago,

The myth of the Battle of the Teutoburg Forest has, in the past, been employed in Germany as a symbol of the nation struggling to defend itself against various occupiers. In A.D. 9, the Teuton, Arminius (also known as 'Hermann'), lured 10,000 Roman soldiers into an ambush and thus prevented the Roman general, Varus, from conquering the territory north of the Rhine. Subsequently, Arminius was instrumentalized as a symbol of the warding off of foreign influences and – in connection with the creation of the German nation state in the 19th century – to emphasize the unity of the German people. The unification of Germany led to the erection of a monumental statue in honour of Arminius, some 50 metres in height, at the highest point in the Teutoburg Forest. However, in the 1980s, the discovery of a Roman face mask and Roman coins led to the realization that Arminius's statue was located some 150 kilometres from the correct spot. The museum that was in turn established at that location – in Kalkriese – was given the name, *Varusschlacht*, after Arminius's adversary, as the name *Hermannsschlacht* (as the Battle of the Teutoburg Forest is referred to in German) was already in use. Due to its unusual design, the museum was discussed in numerous prestigious architecture journals, but failed to attract large numbers of visitors. It is not exciting enough without the *myth*. Nevertheless, an attempt has been made, with the help of Playmobil Romans, pop concerts, firework displays and extensive merchandising, to provide the appropriate experience. One of the museum's best-selling products is a small salami with the name, *Harter Hermann* (Hard Hermann). With this sausage from the battlefield, the museum has thus, aided by a large dose of imagination, yielded to the (human) need for myths.

Observation in the context of the project
THE LIMES ROMANUS, THE FUTURE OF HISTORY,
2006

the Romans and Batavi were much better than we at living in harmony with the landscape, is, however, something which could be used and made visible. The Romans and Batavi established settlements on the more elevated backs of creeks, not the less elevated backlands, where they let their livestock graze until the water came. This self-explanatory method, which is still reflected on geomorphological maps, has not been in use here since dikes were constructed to enclose the area. In the project **THE LIMES ROMANUS, THE FUTURE OF HISTORY** (2006), the Juurlink + Geluk firm of landscape architects used the geomorphological map of the area to determine how the landscape park should be used in future. On the backs of the creeks, they projected infrastructure and the more intensive recreational facilities, and on the backlands, the less intensive facilities and run-off areas. If such an approach were applied, in the course of time, the logic of the subsoil would again become visible and conform to how the area was used formerly.

SOIL-ARCHIVE LANDSCAPE

Although it is possible to allow certain selected features in the landscape, which refer to certain specific periods, to play dominant roles, by definition, the landscape contains, hidden within it, an entire stratification of different historical layers. Picking out and 'bringing to life' one historic stratum, with the relevant historical reference as legitimization, is an act of sheer arbitrariness. Rather than endlessly quibbling about the true facts of a situation and how to visualize it, in order to be able to refer to it in our current concept, we should actually be celebrating the dynamics from which landscape comes about. And cultural heritage plays a variety of roles in these dynamics. For example, the Valletta Treaty obliges us to inventory and, if possible, make secure, all hidden treasures encountered prior to making any intervention in the land. As a standard feature, archaeologists always draw up 'archaeological probability maps' for the entire area in

question prior to such interventions. However, according to archaeologists, there is no such thing as an entirely 'archaeology-free' area. At any given location, valuable artefacts could be lying under the ground, which is why we can speak of a 'soil archive'. It is not the aim of archaeologists to dig up everything. They prefer to preserve artefacts where they are found. This makes certain demands, or to put it more correctly, places certain limits on how far one can go in developing the landscape. When we allow this respect for these specific limitations to dominate the designing process, a rich palette of soil-archive landscapes develops; such a culture-historical approach in turn gives rise to new landscapes, ones that are without any precedent or historical reference, but rather, entirely new.

REASSURING, INVENTED HISTORY

History can also be used to ward off the future. In the late 1990s, the Municipality of Potsdam refused a project developer permission to build an apartment complex at an attractive spot on the River Havel. The resourceful developer then discovered in the municipal archives that, until 1945, a baroque church, the Heilig-Geist-Kirche, had stood at the very same spot, and commissioned his architect to model the apartment complex as best he could after it. Under the pretext that he would be restoring a historic situation, the developer obtained a building permit without any difficulty.

The Netherlands, too, can boast some superb examples of historicizing project development. An entire genesis from the year 1000 was, for example, invented to make possible a new residential area near the town of Assen. This 'history', which contained elements that typically form part of the history of settlements in the region in question, was written by the keeper of the municipal archives himself. The entire history was faked-to-measure in accordance with a desired, and for the developer feasible, end-result, which in turn makes the story so extremely authentic for our time, in which it is, after all, not a question of *whether* one will be screwed – of that one can be sure –, but

THE THEATRE OF DIGGING

Archaeology first really comes to life when it is 'in action', that is to say, when archaeologists actually start excavating and finds are actually made. In Lingezegen Park (now under construction), a number of archaeological finds have been made, and many more are expected. It nevertheless does not appear a sensible idea to go about reconstructing Roman history here, firstly, because extremely little is known about the type of habitation that has taken place in the area, and, second, because the soil contains numerous temporal strata, each with its own story and value. Ensuring the permanent presence of archaeological digging here, and ensuring that these are accessible to the public, would allow the area's history to occupy a vital place, in respect both of how it is experienced and actively remembered.

Perception in the context of the project
THE LIMES ROMANUS, THE FUTURE OF HISTORY,
2006

rather, the quality of the screwing. Even the name Kloosterveste for the new area was fictional. That the land was once owned by a monastery, *was* based on fact, but no evidence had been found for a monastery ever having started a settlement there. Names bearing historical references also have a reassuring effect on prospective residents and future home-buyers, which is primarily why their use is now so fashionable in connection with (proposed) processes of change.

If one considers that the role of cultural heritage in spatial developments is by definition dependent on interpretation, one can look at the current trend of historicizing construction with a smile on one's face. In any case, one can conclude that a large group of home-buyers pay attention to history. Not only does the market produce substantial quantities of homes in the fashionable style of the 1930s, but also, for example, much newbuild with authentic Zaan-Region details in Noord-Holland and Brabantian homes with village-dignitary connotations in Brabant. Construction technology makes it possible: once the concrete shell is complete, a sauce bearing a reference to the history of one's choice can be poured over it as a finish.

PARQUETTING

The construction of a home, neighbourhood or building is essentially the realization of an ideal which, during the designing process, was developed as an idea. However, society changes too quickly for ideals to be able to become reality. Realized utopias are sometimes already obsolete by the time they are completed, and usually so inflexible that they rapidly qualify for demolition, or are exchanged for the next current designs which at that moment still seem utopian. The city never ceases to move and change in the course of time. It is not an ideal end-product, but rather, a constant succession of interim products which can neither be designed on the drawing table nor realized all at once. Nevertheless, this is what frequently happens when new urban areas are designed: the factors, time and the human being, are eliminated due to economic-organizational considerations. To ensure that time does exert an influence, I developed, in the early 1990s, the principle of parquetting, which can enable even a contextless new town like Almere to make history.

The parquetting principle simulates time. The parquetting principle is a game enabling multiple ideals to enter into competition with one another. The competition results in a landscape containing the fragments of unattained ideals. By taking this imperfect landscape as a starting point for the new settlement, one creates a need on the part of the settlement constantly to reconsider itself. With the help of simulation, entirely new plans can develop. In future, these plans will be able to adjust to constantly changing demands, as they were also once shaped by history during the design process, and had to demonstrate flexibility in the course of their development. As a result, history is not just referred to, used or invented, but rather *made* by the interested parties (see further pp 116-135).

ALMERE, SQUATTERS' QUARTER

In the late 1970s and early 1980s, a movement was active across Europe that demonstrated its opposition to illegitimate practices involving speculation with residential housing and house vacancy, by occupying houses. The government dealt firmly with the movement; most of the squatted premises were cleared. With the help of new laws and plans, though, many of the ideas espoused by the squatters' movement nevertheless found their way into new government policy.
A recent development in many newbuild areas has been an intensive search for an identity, whereby old architectural styles are copied with great industry and enthusiasm. As a token of respect for the squatters' movement and the consciousness it brought about, the shift in society it caused could, in the context of this identity quest, be given a fitting conclusion if some of the important buildings demolished during the squatter era were re-erected and a squatters' quarter created from them. The Dutch new town of Almere would be the perfect place for such a project. Since its founding in the 1970s, Almere has slowly been building up its own history. By realizing these original squatters' premises, Almere could quickly create a very important history for itself, and one of great significance for it.

Proposal, 1993

68

Parquette landscape, 1991. Photo: Thea van den Heuvel

OPPORTIMISM

Acting in an authentic manner in development processes does not call for a purely scientific approach, exclusively focussed on obtaining the 'truth', but rather, an opportunistic approach with an optimistic streak. We must not hold on to the illusion that we can even approximately determine 'the truth' about historical situations of which we only possess fragments and for which we may have only one single source. It is not actually germane whether we know a great deal or very little about a situation in the past; any opinion we might form about it is doomed to be off the mark. Rather than acting as though this is not the case, it would be better to embrace the situation, and approach history's neces-sary role opportunistically/optimistically, or *opportimistically*.

History and remnants of cultural heritage can play a wide variety of roles in the current and future space – from legitimatising current actions to warding off the future. Historical references are of great value for determining our temporal position. They locate us in a tradition and, in so doing, confirm a continuity and demark our expectation of a future. China's enormous present construction boom at the beginning of the 20th century exhibits interesting rele-vant examples. Although, where the construction of office buildings is concerned, architectural experimentation has the upper hand, in residential construction, the accent is on the (western) past. In China, that type of historical referencing has now taken on a life of its own. 'China is catching up with the world', is how a sales man-ager in the computer field in Xiamen summed it up. The extended period of isolation the country has experienced, in combination with its sudden prosperity, is inspiring a potpourri of architectural references, enabling the country to bring world history under its own roof and clearly to declare that it now forms part of it.

Despite the great value history has for our present-day built environment, it is not possible to identify one single proper way to ap-proach it in the constant process of spatial change. References made purely to values that things had in the past are, in any case, insufficient. Cultural heritage can only be of value to us if its value is of our time.

AUTHENTIC

STRENGTHENING THROUGH WEAKENING

Over the past fifty years the dikes along the major rivers have suffered from improvement and have, as a result, been damaged by the supposed upgrading of the dikes. For those entrusted with their upkeep, plant cover on the dikes was for a long time a sign of their strength. Plant cover ensured that the dike didn't crumble from the beating of the waves during floods. Over the course of the previous century, however, this plant cover has been cultivated more and more. Plant cover meant grass, and grass was increasingly refined. So much so that at one time the dike made for a better football surface (apart from the slope of course) than many an official pitch, but the plant cover no longer performed its proper function. Refinement meant that the grass rooted at just one depth and therefore it hardly strengthened the dike at all. The remedy for this was called weakening. No more fertilizing and removing the mown grass. The effect was a more resilient and much more diverse plant cover that rooted at many more depths. So a clever neglect of the situation produced much stronger dikes.

Observation based on the project
THE INVENTION OF THE FLOOD PLAIN MODEL,
2000

Not so very long ago geographical conditions combined with available building materials to define the architecture of a place. The site chosen for construction and the materials at hand, such as wood, stone, marble or trash, were decisive factors in determining the appearance and size of a structure. Cultural historians and tourist associations in particular still celebrate these original dynamics of creation of the built environment. In reality, however, this has all become folklore now. After all, we are now able to build what we want to anywhere and we no longer celebrate the clever way we deal with the limitations of a place, but rather, applaud the endless possibilities available to us. The difficult thing about such almost endless possibilities is that the identity of a situation, its very particularity, no longer becomes manifest through our struggle with the limitations, but rather, is created and added after the event, as it were. Despite our enthusiasm about these endless possibilities, the purifying, the refining and the individualizing influence that limitations can have on a certain structure or landscape are nevertheless increasingly missed.

LIVING ON ARTIFICIAL WATER

We see fantastic reactions to this deficiency, particularly in today's booming economies such as China and Dubai. Unique built structures created as a result of a difficult struggle with the limitations of one place, Europe for example, are transported in their entirety to a totally different place where those same limitations usually don't apply. If desired, the limitations are simply recreated. This fascinating principle in current urban planning is very clearly evident in the coastal development in Dubai. Fifteen years ago the country had a coastline of less than 64 kilometres. The construction of spectacular residential islands in the territorial waters off the coast will soon increase the length of the coastline to no fewer than 820 kilometres. Economic growth and technical developments mean that possibilities are unlimited. One of the trends on these artificial islands is living on water. Almost all new forms of this in Dubai are designed, built and

LIMITATIONS

Wetland by MG Architects, **AMPHIBIOUS LIVING** prize winner.

sold by the Dutch. And that's no coincidence. The geographical location of two-thirds of the Netherlands below sea level, the rivers that slice the country, and the marshy soil mean that Dutch urban planning and architecture enjoys a long tradition in dealing with water. But despite this long tradition, dealing with the real limitations of particular sites in the Netherlands scarcely plays any role in the creation of unique urban landscapes.

AMPHIBIOUS LIVING

Up until the 1960s the dynamics of water were a natural fact. When, for example, you built a house in an area susceptible to flooding, you didn't put down a parquet floor in your living room; you used flagstones instead. If the water came in, you carried the furniture upstairs and moved in with family. When the water subsided, you scrubbed the floor and put the furniture back in place. From the

1960s onwards, there was a growing belief in the Netherlands in the technical ability to control water. As a result, water became increasingly unimportant when it came to choosing a building location. In 2005 the minister responsible even went so far as to say that it was a 'huge challenge' to build at the lowest point on the Netherlands, even if that lowest point lies more than six metres below sea level. Water, once an enemy, now seems to be a friend, and there is an increasing discrepancy between our awareness of the genuine dynamics of water and its image of them.

In many new Dutch residential areas the boggy soil is scarcely a factor any more. Two metres of sand are simply spread on top to stabilize the weak soil and then construction can begin. But in more recent times water still manages to make its way to the surface. To win the favour of house-buyers, people go to great lengths to produce individuality, authenticity and identity in new residential areas. Oddly enough, these are not sought in the landscape where construction takes place, but devised afterwards. Once all the problems of exploitation, plot division, infrastructure and water management have been tackled, it's time to start thinking about identity. That's when the landscape elements or original qualities of the location can start to play a role again, although just in a manageable and symbolic manner. Water is then only too readily used as an image in places where in fact it could play a much more fundamental role.

In Gouda, roads have been built for decades on soggy soil, only for them to sink again and again. Because of the fixation on the road surface, roads are raised time and time again, and now there are absurd road walls here and there that often extend as far down as twelve metres.

On the basis of this idea, in 2000 I developed the project **AMPHIBIOUS LIVING**, in which a number of possible new icons for living and water were defined. Amphibious homes lie on the ground when it's dry and float when the water arrives. **AMPHIBIOUS LIVING** is therefore a call to no longer compulsively control the ground and water. It is a call for admitting the influence of the weather, the tides and seasons in the residential environment and, at the same time, for a new residential mentality. So it is precisely on the basis of those limitations of marshiness and water problems that unique new icons can be created (see further pp 152-163).

SOCIALLY ACCEPTABLE LIVING
ON ESTATE-AGENT'S WATER

In an increasing number of new residential districts, space is reserved for floating dwellings in areas with overblown titles like Water Gardens, Blue City or Golden Coast. The ponds and canals in the new residential districts are also referred to derisively as 'estate-agent water'. Owing to the mortgage possibilities and a number of completed water villas by renowned architects like Herman Hertzberger and Art Zaaijer, living on water is no longer the realm of adventurers and DIY'ers and has become socially acceptable and, especially, very suitable for the housing market because of the suggestion of freedom and independence

LIGHTHOUSE DWELLINGS

The new neighbourhood of Carnisselande was built in Barendrecht, just to the south of Rotterdam. During the preparatory phase the quality of the soil was insufficiently studied to fully map the marsh on which the neighbourhood was to be built. Studies of the results of drilling operations resulted in traces of an old creek being mistaken for a thick layer of peat. This layer of 'thick water' then caused sewage drains placed on Friday to sunk out of sight by the following Monday. On the same location as the vanished sewage pipe, a series of light tower dwellings were built as an easily marketable identity of the place and to represent the connection with the water. So here we had a relation first denied, then struggled against and finally represented in an absurd manner.

Observation based on the project
AMPHIBIOUS LIVING, 2000

74

that comes with the idea of living on water. Bobbing up and down, the dwellings can, if desired, turn to face the sun or even locate somewhere completely different. The reality, of course, is different. The plots are usually so tight that there's not much turning possible; the dwellings are usually fitted with all modern conveniences and therefore totally dependent on the umbilical chord of amenities at their berthing place. Such berthing places are limited in number and therefore the home cannot just moor anywhere, not to mention the often insurmountable obstacles of bridges, dams and dikes that the home would encounter on its journey from one place to the next. The freedom and independence from the sales brochures are therefore based suggestion, but that is exactly the level at which they best function. The residents of the floating homes are, as a rule, very attached to their comfort and certainty. What they essentially seek is the impression of independence and the feeling of freedom without having to bear the negative consequences of it.

By now it's the government that is starting to discover the genuine identity-furnishing power of water. Water is not just a surface; it also has a bottom. Decades of agricultural poison have often rendered this very polluted. Interesting alternatives to the expensive process of dredging and removal are devised. Wrapping up the dredger and building traditional habitable knolls in flood areas results in identity based on solving a problem. Experiments are also stimulated of late in the river forelands. In the knowledge that the total control of water can no longer be maintained, the Dutch government is commissioning studies into how living and unstable water levels can go hand in hand. The river forelands are the perfect trial area for this.

CHEMICAL HERITAGE

Our construction technology has become so refined that we can actually build the same way everywhere, and local materials and tradition only return as decoration and illustration. The tools used are the same the whole world over. But almost every situation contains hidden possibilities to enable individualizing limitations to once again exert a strong influence in a self-evident manner on the process of creation. These possibilities that stem from limitations are best revealed through examples, from poisonous to edible.

Every kind of (agricultural) poison that is sprayed on the land and is washed away into the ditches or whatever is dumped straight into the ditches is stored in the sludge. As a result of what is often a lack of dredging, some Dutch ditches store over thirty years of chemical history. We can therefore rightly speak of 'chemical heritage'. It is the legacy of the activities that have brought is affluence, nut also the heritage of long years of careless use of land. Now polluted sludge is a big problem even when it's stored in the ditches, but it's a much bigger problem once it's dredged and has to be disposed on as chemical waste. Nonetheless, many regions have to find a solution for the problem of sludge.

75

There is a whole series of new processing methods for the widest possible range of pollutants. Sludge can be processed in an absolutely safe way in the production landscape itself and, moreover, has the potential to enrich the cultural landscape. Through the deployment of plants to process poisonous substances, sludge processing can take on the role of maintaining or restoring certain landscape characteristics that have been lost. The chemical heritage that lies stored in the ditch sludge turns out to be of an unexpected richness. Not only does the legibility of the history make it rich, but also and especially the unsuspected landscape possibilities that lie hidden in the processing of the sludge.

GRILLWALKER

That laws and practical objections can aid the fulfilment of a dream is illustrated by the case of a sausage seller on the streets of Berlin. In the late 1990s this man dreamed of his own takeaway to sell sausages. You couldn't find a better place for that in Berlin than Alexanderplatz, and so the entrepreneur tried to build up the common law at that location by first establishing himself again and again, first on the ground and later on supports, under a parasol and with a tent. But his intentions were grasped by those who maintain law and order; a licence to sell sausages doesn't mean a licence for a particular location. The ambulant jewellery sellers who can acquire a licence for their 'belly shop' give him the idea to become mobile with his grill and accessories. Once he has successfully dealt with all the problems of the weight of the contraption, the safety of the gas over buckled around him, and the hygienic threat from the birds overhead, the Grillwalker became reality. Now the Grillwalker has been approved by the TÜV and admitted in all countries of the European Union. The Grillwalker functions with two people. While one of them grills the sausages and keeps moving all the time, the other ensure a continuous supply of fresh wares from a coolbox mounted on a bicycle. Grillwalkers are a rage and you can hardly find an important public place or event in Berlin without seeing one.

PROBLEMS ARE FUTURE ICONS

Many of the previous examples have the potential to develop into icons. Icons are sought after in many spatial plans to provide added conviction to the desired result of a long and toilsome process of change. You can penetrate in the process of creation by realizing that the icons of today were in fact the problems of yesterday. On the site of the Oostvaardersplassen (a big nature reserve in the IJsselmeer polders), for example, the state planners actually wanted to create a site for heavy industry. The area turned out to be too wet and nature *unfortunately* developed far too fast, the upshot of which was that an icon suddenly came into being. Likewise, the typical polder landscape was never devised on the basis of aesthetic, tourist or iconographic motives, but

FARMER AS CULTURAL-HISTORICAL CONSTANT

Many people see in a farmer a food producer at the mercy of the regulations of the world market and Brussels who, trapped in a vicious circle of business innovation and scaling up just keeps going. But instead, we should actually see him as someone who produces things in the agrarian landscape for the surrounding towns, such as food, care, openness, nature and recreation. That would open up a world of new production possibilities. Seen in that light, the farmer is in fact the most important cultural-historical constant in the countryside. Not in the form of a farmer from the post-war era of reconstruction, the post-war industrial agrarian who refine his production with all sorts of technical innovations, even if that is at the expense of the landscape; but as the farmer of a century ago who wanted to produce and had to do that in a difficult landscape with lots of limitations. To that end he devised inventive interventions on a small scale that produced the landscape that we now consider the most valuable cultural landscape of Holland. Not a landscape created on the drawing board that was constructed in one go with big machines and then had to be maintained at great cost, but a landscape made with a lot of sensitivity and evolves continually with every new ambition and problem related to usefulness, passion and individualization.

Observation based on the project
KRABBEPLAS VLAARDINGEN, 2008
Thanks to Jan Duijndam.

76

only serve to turn marshy land into cultivated land on which one could then earn a living. The historical cultural landscapes that we now consider worthy of protection, were never created with that in mind. Taking the qualities of the cultural landscape and other cultural-historical phenomena into consideration when make planning decisions is today an unmistakeably conscious choice for a limitation. If we cease to deny those limitations when solving problem but rather make them the key element in the process of change, then the icons of the future will emerge.

HAPPY CRAB

The most beautiful things can be born out of misunderstandings. Even if these misunderstandings are created on purpose. Almost no one knows it, but the Krabbeplas (Crab Lake) recreation area in Midden-Delfland is named after engineer G. Krabbe. The lake was originally made for surfing, but this sport isn't popular any more. But it function all the better as a local marsh: it grows and acquires more and more functions for water purification, cane production and the accommodation of threatened fauna. The lake could even present itself as an asylum for mitten crabs, a species of animal that is advancing undesirably in surface water. The mitten crabs caught elsewhere can be delivered within a specially fenced off area of the former surfing lake. A programme for cultivation and refinement could then be set up to service foreign customers. The Krabbeplas restaurant is renamed The Happy Crab and specialized in crab recipes, which by then becomes known as 'Midden-Delfland crab', a recognized local product. Chinese tourists can enjoy their lunch here on the way from Kinderdijk to Amsterdam. And the Krabbeplas acquires a new origin with retrospective effect.

Observation based on the project
KRABBEPLAS VLAARDINGEN, 2008

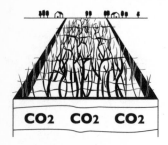

CLIMATE FARMER

Farming is a hard life. No so much on account of all that drudgery with the unyielding soil but, increasingly, on account of all that drudgery with unyielding bureaucracy, expressed in fertilizer regulations, production regulations, world market regulations, and landscape regulations. Farmers, however, are proving to be exceptionally resilient and increasingly shift their focus to other products that they can provide on their land. We have, for example, the climate farmer, who deals with issues that are the direct or indirect result of the influence of a changing climate on the cultural landscape. These farmers can offer solutions for the problems of the city, such as water retention, peak retention, and water purification. Processing polluted dredging or generating energy present challenges that can boost the landscape *and* the income of farmers. Farmers on peaty soil can even consider themselves to be climate farmers. For research has shown that the burning of peat as a result of draining – a natural process that always occurs during impoldering with a fixed low water level – accounts for some five percent of the Dutch national CO_2 output. A flexible water level, or even the establishment of a fixed high water level, reduces or even stops the peat burning and, hence, the CO_2 output. That helps our environment and helps us achieve the Kyoto targets, and deserves to be rewarded financially. Cane can then be cultivated on the soggy soil. That benefits nature, roofs and, because of the burning, the generation of energy.

Observation within the framework of the project **KRABBEPLAS VLAARDINGEN**, 2008

Identity is a broad term, open to numerous definitions and interpretations. The phenomenon of identity is no longer strictly 'territorial', or rather, it is no longer determined by the place you come from. Your ancestry, profession or region does not define identity any more; instead, it is increasingly the case that you 'identify with something'. Identity has become a verb. You do not acquire it; you choose it, compose it yourself. What's more, one person can possess a multitude of identities today. Consequently, a person's identity has become much more intangible. Needless to say, the surroundings where someone lives, works and relaxes are still prime ingredients in how that identity is composed. Nevertheless, a broad array of current phenomena spanning the full breadth of culture supplement and strengthen this identity. And this is equally true of cities that are searching for an identity of their own. They often look for it in their historical quarters, even if they don't exist, or in past events and situations that made the city what it is today. Often they only have eyes for the pleasant aspects, the preferred history, beautiful things. In doing so, they risk overlooking precisely those qualities that offer most potential. Delays, garbage and struggle in particular can hide strong identities.

IDENTITY IS NOT NICE

When it comes to identity, cities usually think of nice, agreeable things, but identity does not necessarily have to be nice to work. It is either strong or weak. That dawned on the new mayor of Tilburg a few years ago. During the nineteenth century the town developed because of the textile industry. One of the products used for colouring and bleaching wool was urine, of the human variety. Workers and their families filled pitchers with urine and exchanged them for payment at the factory. That's why the people were known for miles around as the 'pitcher pissers'. All the townspeople gradually embraced the nickname, and now it has become the key symbol of the city's annual carnival. But the mayor wished only the best for his city's citizens, and he

IS A VERB

therefore resolutely rejected what he considered was this 'disgusting symbol of the suppressed worker who carried his urine to the factory to boost his earnings a little'. Instead, the mayor wanted to present Tilburg as a pleasant green city, wonderfully located on the water, with a village-like ambiance that offered the amenities of a city, easily accessible by all modes of transport yet tranquilly remote, and, above all, in the centre of Europe! The people contemplated covering the mayor in tar and feathers and dragging him out of the city, because the pisser symbol turned out to be the most cherished symbol of local identity.

ANOTHER NATIVENESS

A feature of our present age is our struggle to deal with the influences of other cultures in European society. This is a major theme among politicians, many of whom claim to be 'native' people who are witnessing 'their' society changing. Politics are scarcely influenced by other cultures, even though other cultures already exert a major influence on our cities. Ethnic groups remain distinct in cities but grow increasingly towards one another. It is clear that integration does not mean that everybody is going to look like the current 'standard-European', in as far as one can speak of that already, but that different groups will borrow traits from one another. Multiculturalism will not come about without a ripple, however. Society will first become 'pluricultural' and then end up as a different 'nativeness'. We can see that process unfolding in those aspects of native identity that seem most unassailable. Take, for example, local dialect. Besides the influence of international TV culture, we see more and more Caribbean terms and Arabian sounds cropping up. Politicians and administrators do their best to ensure that the 'transition' proceeds smoothly. To that end, they shop around among the phenomena of cultures for elements that are not scary but appealing and, hence, reassuring.

HINDUSTANIZATION AS PHANTOM IDENTITY

The Transvaal district in The Hague is currently undergoing a sweeping reconstruction that involves a lot of demolition and

DETENTION LAND

Detention land is a proposal to breathe new life into the tradition of the penal colony as a humane form of captivation. This penal colony will be built off the Dutch coast near the Hook of Holland and consists of a series of towers whose plans take the shape of numbers. Over the years, the inmates will work from these towers to reclaim land from the sea in strips that belong to the differently numbered buildings. The size of the area of reclaimed land in these strips, as well as the height of the buildings, is of no importance for the legibility of the code and can be extended at will. The prison can set up its own system for producing food, run by the detainees. A port, an airport, and companies can also locate there. After sitting out his term, the ex-prisoner can acquire a piece of land at a reduced price. A culture in which people can develop self-initiative, where work is available, and where all inhabitants share responsibility for maintaining the land they themselves have helped to reclaim – all this ensures that prisoners integrate well into the penal colony and makes rehabilitation on the mainland easier, and perhaps even superfluous. The initial isolation will gradually give way to a full-fledged society that shapes its own identity and, accordingly, undoes its own isolation.

Proposal for the
Government Buildings Agency, 1994

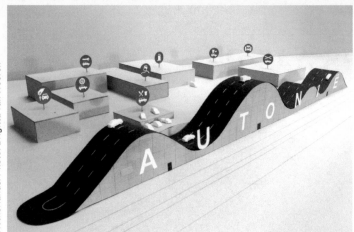

AUTONIA proposal for Transvaal district in The Hague, Netherlands. Photo: Brigitta van Weeren

TESAMEHEID

When the Transvaal neighbourhood was built in The Hague in the early twentieth century, the Boer Wars in South Africa had just ended. The Boers were descendents of Dutch settlers, and their heroic battle against the English oppressors was celebrated in many places around the Netherlands. One such place was the neighbourhood in The Hague that acquired the name Transvaal and where the streets were given geographical and historical references to that part of the world. A whole series of streets were named after 'heroic' Boer soldiers, the very same Boers who later laid the foundations for apartheid.

Now, however, the neighbourhood is no longer an ethnic reflection of the African Boers. Instead, it has become extremely pluricultural and diverse. Because the neighbourhood is populated by low-income groups, the local housing association views this diversity as undesirably one-sided. By demolishing cheap housing and replacing it with more expensive housing, the housing association is hoping to make the neighbourhood more diverse. The imbalance deemed so undesirable and negative is being tackled in this way. Here, in the neighbourhood named after the founding fathers of apartheid, an anti-apartheid policy based on income is being applied, in fanatic pursuit of a cultural mingling deemed desirable and that, in the spirit of the Boers, you could call 'Tesameheid'.

Observation within the framework of the Laboratory of the interim, 2008

newbuild activity. Though the multi-ethnic character of the neighbourhood is indisputably one of its most important features, it does little to attract tourists or foster the desired socio-economic progress. The municipality therefore, prompted by a couple of striking Hindustan shops, decided to market the neighbourhood as an 'icon of Hindustan culture'. Yet the reality is that many Hindustan residents are moving out of the neighbourhood and being replaced by eastern European and Turkish people. A 'Hindu Street', however, makes for a better unique selling point than 'the umpteenth multicultural shopping street', and the newly constructed Hindustan-Oriental image lends itself well to marketing campaigns. After all, it opens up a wealth of possible positive images: golden elephants, coloured herbs, stunning Indian women, exuberant parties, tropical beaches and so on. But the predominantly Turkish businessmen who now run shops in Transvaal must undergo a course in Hindustanization to conform to the desired picture. And so the local authority deliberately propagates a phantom identity. It holds up certain characteristics to be true, even though they have not been significant or even present for a long time, as the true identity.

AUTONIA

In light of what the current identity of Transvaal could be, and which, besides, could exert a culturally connecting effect in the future, the phenomenon of the car immediately springs to mind. For when it comes to cars, everybody hails from Autonia, but the car is scarcely recognized as a cultural phenomenon. Despite the fact that there is hardly another activity subject to more restrictions, driving is the ultimate symbol of freedom and status. The car is not only a mode of transport but also a proud possession and extension of one's identity. The municipality doesn't see it that way, however, and ignores the power of the car as a cultural connector. The actions around the car (refuelling, washing, tinkering with the engine) are deliberately separated and accommodated on what are often unattractive sites or industrial zones where it's impossible to show off your car. AUTONIA is a proposal

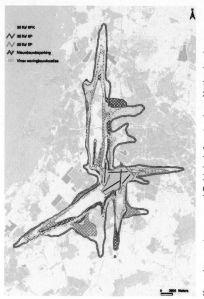

Kerosine contour around Schiphol, Amsterdam, Netherlands.
Source: www.geluidsnet.nl

to create a special place of encounter in Transvaal centred on the car and, in the process, to upgrade dilapidated commercial areas in the district and give them a more appealing appearance.

KEROSINE CONTOUR

'Negative' phenomena can have a positive influence on how space is planned. Schiphol Airport, close to Amsterdam, seen as an important engine of the Dutch economy, succeeds in doing that in its own way. Air transport plays a fundamental and irrevocable role in international travel and, accordingly, in our culture – not only as a hip round-the-clock city, hub or shopping centre, but also at a much bigger scale. On account of safety and environmental requirements, planes taking off and landing have to fly over uninhabited areas as much as possible. The uninhabited areas around Schiphol Airport therefore form something of a kerosine contour that carves out a big area in the chockfull province of Noord-Holland. Initiatives such as the protection of what's known as the 'Oer-IJ', the term used to denote the last remaining area of the original estuary around Amsterdam, benefit from this. Despite being located directly beneath the approach route to the Polderbaan runway, it is unlikely that this geographical monument will be eroded further in size by new housing or commercial development. In that way, the expansion of Schiphol is helping to safeguard the vital open landscape in the most densely populated part of the Netherlands, and a side effect of its growth is the protection against any further loss of the past.

RECYCLE VALLEY

Defining the cultural qualities of the locality was the key concern in the project **THE DISCOVERY OF THE FLOOD PLAIN MODEL** in Beuningen in Gelderland in 2000. The region was proud of its distinctive

PLANESPOTTER AVENUE

To protect the city and air traffic, the surroundings of airports that are developed are subject to special restrictions in terms of the maximum building heights in the approach and departure zones of the runways. For the city of Berlin, these can be read on the map 'Bauschutzbereiche der Flughäfen' (Senatsverwaltung für Bau- und Wohnungswesen Berlin, 1994). This map renders visible an infrastructure that we normally, from the ground, can only perceive in fragments. In the proposal **VOLATILE URBANISM**, the many visitors who reach the city from the air will be welcomed in a fitting manner. A so-called 'Planespotter avenue' will be created directly beneath the eastern approach route to Berlin's Tegel Airport. The lamps will shine in two directions: downwards to illuminate the street and upwards to create texts legible from the air, from inside the planes. Texts like: 'Welcome to Berlin', and the latest news or messages from sponsors.

Proposal for Berlin, 1997

houses built of bricks baked from river clay from the local flood plains. Almost all the brick factories had closed down, and construction materials were now bought at the local DIY shop, with no connection to the region at all. But the project revealed that the original dynamism of building with local materials was still potentially very much alive – no longer with brick but with reused waste material. A big waste incineration plant has been located on the border between Beuningen and Nijmegen for as long as anyone can remember. Transport routes by road and water made it a suitable site. It is referred to informally as the 'Arse of Nijmegen'. In recent years, however, an increasing number of companies opened up around the incineration plant and started reusing the waste. 2012Architecten charted the new flows of material and named the new raw materials created. Emerging here is a new specialism that we called 'Recycle Valley'. Waste becomes building material, turning the arse into a mouth. And the region can get going once again with its own building material.

We have a tendency to view the history of development as a 'sacred story' and like to emphasize the positive sides of the past. For no matter how bad it was, we managed to survive. When it comes to archaeological finds, for example, we usually think of valuable material, even though the majority of valuable finds do, in fact, consist of waste. We shouldn't have too many romantic notions of what landscape was in the Roman era or in the Middle Ages. Landscape was simply land not yet cultivated; wilderness that was downright dangerous on account of its unpredictability and plunderers. Our past is also made up of 'dark sides' and 'unpleasant' cultural history.

Those who manage processes of change usually harp on about how we should focus on the possibilities and not the problems in situations subject to change. That shifts the view/perspective from problem solving to the inviting perspective, despite the fact that it is precisely within the problems that wonderful opportunities await discovery. The unique way in which the Dutch landscape deals with water is a good example. The dikes, the polders and the town canals were only created because water was a problem that needed to be solved before people could achieve their ambitions. Many towns cherish their castles and ramparts, even though they were only built to keep out the enemy. That heritage would never have been created were it not for the threat of the enemy. Today, too, problems still offer the best potential for producing new identities.

DESIGN

THE LIFTED LIFT-BRIDGE

Rotterdam is proud to be seen as a 'city of work', one where all noses dynamically point toward one thing: progress. It is a city that does not bask in 'past results', as these do not guarantee future performance. Nevertheless, the symbols of the dynamic, forward-looking mentality Rotterdam has inherited from its past can count on a nostalgic treatment. An example of this is the renowned lift bridge, De Hef, which has lain idly on the sidelines since 24 September 1993, when Rotterdam's underground rail connection was opened to the public. The old railway bridge now functions as a reminder of the spot from which trains departed from the city centre, but does cost one million euro per year in unemployment benefit, as the bridge's steel construction and mechanism are perpetually maintained in perfect condition.

A few kilometres away, developments around the Rijnhaven, Maashaven and Waalhaven are rapidly taking form. To improve connections between the Wilhelmina Pier, Katendrecht and Charlois, new bridges are being designed – whilst nearby, one of Rotterdam's proudest bridges lies unemployed. What could be closer to the essence of Rotterdam than taking the lift bridge, De Hef, and moving it to the Maashaven. There, this monument, having had its function restored, could shine again and provide a seamless link between nostalgia and progress.

Proposal, **THE DISCOVERY OF THE MAAS RIVER PLAIN**, for Kunst op Zuid, 2009

In 2001, at the invitation of the Bergen School of Architecture in Norway, I visited the coastal island of Utsira. Just getting to the island turned out to be quite an ordeal. This great broken-off piece of rock could only be reached with a small ferry boat, which had a tough time negotiating the spectacular waves here. The small island, 2 km across, had two harbours. Whilst, due to the wind and the rough water caused by it, the ferry boat was unable to enter the harbour on the one side of the island, it was luckily able to do so on the other. The wind also played a dominant role in the planning and development of the island, or rather, their prevention. There was, for example, hardly a tree to be found; every attempt by a tree to take root here had been thwarted by the cruel wind. Except for one tree, which had made its courageous bid behind the local church. The small building had kept the tree out of the wind, making it possible for it to grow in freedom. When the tree had become so tall that its branches began to rise above the roof of the little church, the wind got its grip on the tree, thus preventing further growth. Because no leaves could grow beyond the edge of the roof, in the course of time, the tree gradually took on the shape of the church, as though nothing could be more normal. The spectacular result of a tree with a 'gable roof' looks at first glance like a somewhat large, artistically trimmed box hedge in a baroque garden, attractive examples of which, created by inventive gardeners, can be found everywhere in the world. With one big difference: this Norwegian house-tree was designed by no one. No one decided how the tree would look. Nor did anyone give the tree its shape out of spite. The tree's shape is a result of the specific character of the natural conditions in which it has grown. And in this way, it is a pre-eminent representative of the identity of the island where it stands. Not because a local artist came up with an idea, leading to its promotion by the island's tourist office, nor because there is a typically Norwegian tradition of creating pointy trees, but purely because of the specific characteristics of the place where it is located.

THE COMMISSION

A tree with a pitched roof on Utsira island, Norway.

THE AMBITION TO GROW

If one wanted to make this spot's well-earned identity the basis
for a recognizable face for the entire island, a number of steps
could be taken. One could trim other trees so that they were also
pointy, but then one would wind up exclusively concentrating on
the shape which resulted from the unique situation described
above. There were, for that matter, hardly any trees at all on the
island, so that it would first be necessary to plant a tree behind
every house capable of keeping a tree out of the wind, but then
one would only be copying the situation which led to this unique
tree shape. If, however, one considers not just what the situation in question brought about, but rather, also *how* the situation
came about, a few things come to mind. The tree was clearly
shaped by the wind. To be more exact, one could say that there
once was a tree with the 'ambition' to grow and whose ambition

89

was accompanied by certain phenomena. Firstly, there was the phenomenon of the harsh wind, which impeded its growth. Then, there was the phenomenon of the little church building, which screened off the tree from the wind. The result is now visible: a tree with a gable roof.

If one wished to continue the quality typical of, and specific to, this tree, one could, rather than copying this specific situation or its specific results, re-apply the unfolding of the situation in the form of ambitions and phenomena. The tree that wants to grow, gets its shape from the object that keeps it out of the wind. One can in turn build fences in one or more shapes, and place trees behind them to be kept out of the wind. In the course of time, this will yield several illustrations of the found principle that is specific to the spot in question. One can then abstract the relevant ambitions and phenomena even further. The tree can be returned to being an object with an ambition to grow, and the phenomena can be labelled as threats or as protection, respectively. The result is as follows: 'a growing object that is under threat takes on the shape of that which protects it', a rule which in turn can be applied to other situations in which the identity of this spot plays a role. In so doing, one continues an essential characteristic of the spot without literally copying it or referring to it.

PAINTED DOOR FITTINGS

On another island off the Norwegian coast, in a small monastery, my attention was drawn to a heavy wooden door with impressive wrought iron fittings. The metal door handle and hinges were generously ornamented with scrolls and frills, but on closer inspection, both handle and hinges appeared to be of very ordinary material and design, and their scrolls and frills to have been painted on them in black. Upon enquiring about the fittings, I was informed that the ambition of the original monks had in fact been for the detailing of their monastery to reflect as much wealth as possible, but that in achieving this ambition, they had been limited by the phenomenon of insufficient funds. The painted door fittings were a result of this. Naturally, one could say that the fittings should actually have been of wrought iron, and that, as soon as the monastic budget permits, the monks should as yet realize the desired situation, as this would be a correct way of expressing their identity in visual form. But in point of fact, the painted fittings already do this with the greatest of precision, such that there is no need for these objects to be replaced. The desire to reflect wealth, combined with an actual lack of it, gave rise to this unique identity, whose continuation need not reside just in the use of painted door fittings, but, for example, in the rule that implements must be provided with a richly decorated appearance using cheap materials.

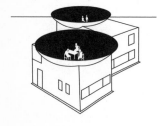

VILLA HORIZON

If you ask house buyers what kind of house they would most like to live in, it turns out not to be a terraced house or an apartment, but a fully detached villa with its own view of the horizon. Across the Netherlands, fully detached villas are as fervently aspired to as they are unattainable. The Netherlands may not yet be full, but a spot with an unobstructed view, with no buildings or other structures on the horizon, where a person can erect his own house, is not at all easy to find in this country.

The Villa Horizon offers people an opportunity to satisfy their wish for their own private horizon. The typology employed here is frequently encountered in areas with sand dunes. The Villa Horizon is a dune pan which, when one reclines in it, takes over one's entire horizon. In this proposal, this aspect has been optimized to such an extent that the Villa Horizon can guarantee everyone his/her own horizon, even in densely populated areas.

Proposal in the context of project
UNDERCOVER, Arnhem, 1997

FIELD OF CHANGE

The unfolding of features typical of and specific to a spot by means of so-called phenomena and ambitions makes it possible to re-use the core aspects of such features without a literal reference to their shape. The manner in which these recognizable features once came about is then dissected into its component parts, and once again deployed in the current situation now undergoing change. In this context, ambitions are the needed or desired interventions that put spatial change into motion. The phenomena do not, in and of themselves, put change into motion, but give colour, direction and guidance to this change. By translating one's analysis of the situation into the various phenomena and ambitions and bringing them together in a table with two coordinates, it is possible to 'draw up a field of change'. I call this field the matrix. It provides an overview of the present situation that is about to change, and all tasks and solutions are enclosed in it.

The matrix plays a role in virtually all of my projects in connection with studying and describing situations. It is from the matrix that the assignment for the change in question emerges. The formulation of this design assignment has grown into something greater than just collecting wishes and identifying and inventorying specific conditions. Before the assignment can be set, all relevant data must first be brought into relation with one another, so that a hierarchy for the process of change can be draughted. The unfolding of the situation in ambitions and phenomena makes it possible to structure the draughting of the assignment as a design process.

The matrix with ambitions and phenomena plays a leading role in **THE MAKING OF**, the concept-development game that emerged from the project **THE INVENTION OF THE FLOOD PLAIN MODEL** in 2001. **THE MAKING OF** is a method for putting a creative thought process in motion amongst the interested parties in a (spatial) process of change. The game enables both professionals and non-professionals to form part of a process of change – not by striving for consensus about the desired end-picture, but through wide involvement in the process of precisely defining the assignment from which that end-picture will emerge (see further pp 164-183).

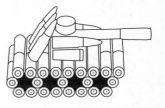

CONTINUITIES

The first train looked like a coach, and another word for a carriage in a train is indeed still *coach*. We still quantify the power of a car's motor in terms of numbers of *horses*. Changes are by definition gradual, and new things always adopt qualities from the phenomena out of which they come. This is in fact necessary, since people need to be able to recognize something before they can accord it recognition. Many newbuild houses, even after Modernism, still resemble classic farmhouses, albeit in a new form, also referred to as 'farmettes'. In the north of Holland, where the farmhouses are traditionally built with a pyramid-roof and are for this reason called *stolpboerderijen* or 'cheese-bell farmhouses', one now sees 'stolperettes' everywhere: newbuild houses with pyramid-roofs. Which is not to say that these houses do not reflect a further stage of development, or that they still must do with the energy supply and sanitary fittings of a hundred years ago. For the ringtone on their iPhones, some people choose the ring of an old dial telephone: a continuity chosen out of spite, that makes using their almost unimaginable digital facilities more approachable. The illustration shows a surprisingly autonomous example of continuity: a tank from the giftshop of the Military Museum in Beijing – built entirely from gold-plated fired bullets.

Perception, 2005

THE PROCESS

Spatial planning is a complicated business. The process of transformation can touch on everything from simple changes to public space, through large-scale restructuring of residential areas, to a regional search for identity. The interests of many people, authorities and businesses must reconcile with the possibilities of the place, its soil and its history. New plans must not only be technically possible and have sufficient support, but they must also be financially viable. Spatial development has been democratized to a great extent with as a result an ever-growing group of interested parties: citizens, authorities, lobby groups, developers, housing associations and sectoral groups. This sometimes leads to constructions never seen before, multitudes of interests with no hierarchy in place, and the lack of a body with final responsibility and supervision. The process is teeming with personal wishes and interests, leading to a result that is a compromise only seldom fulfilling any of its expectations.

I have designed a game plan in THE MAKING OF to break open this kind of process. THE MAKING OF is a method to stimulate the creative thinking process between the concerned *and* the interested parties of a process of (spatial) change. The game allows both professionals and non-professionals to take part in the process of change. It brings together the (many) parties involved while at the same time informing and consulting them as participants so as to become a part of the future changes. The game gives the spatial planners the knowledge and opinion of residents, which gives them in turn a much broader support base. It offers residents insight into and knowledge about the complexity of the task, and also enables them to express their opinion in words other than 'nice' or 'ugly'. Making the ingredients available to all those involved in the field allows everyone the opportunity to come up with their own 'best idea' for the changes.

OF CHANGE

IDEA CONCEPT PLAN

Spatial developments go through various phases; I see three main ones. The first phase, the idea phase, identifies as many possible outcomes and ambitions that do or could play a role in the context of a given situation. During the idea phase, we hand out research assignments, listen to experts and specialists in the context of talks, round-tables or debates, and make analyses of archive material and organize surveys. Even information that seems to have little to do with the subject is brought into the inventory. We research themes that are fascinating and could potentially offer direction. At the same time, a map comes together of how and where certain phenomena could land. It is essential not to discriminate between information in this first phase. At the same time, analyses can never be limited to one discipline, but should come from as many disciplines as possible. No matter how open and broadly oriented professionals are, their analyses tend to be directed at their own professional field. Landscape architects are most aware of landscape, urban planners of the urban fabric, sociologists of human behaviour, and architects of architecture.

All the information from the first phase is collected and divided as much as possible into clusters according to content and theme. The whole package of opinions, wishes, initiatives, threats, and necessary interventions around the situation is thereby collected and then divided into two groups. We call the first group the 'ambitions': these will allow for change in the future. They are necessary or desired initiatives, such as more houses or roads, but can also look towards a desired change in mentality about something such as automobile use. Ambitions start off the process of change in land use. The other group are the so-called phenomena: these do not bring change in and of themselves, but give colour, direction and leadership to the change. An important phenomenon, for example, is the cultural history of the land, and changes must take it into account. But also the need to build up support for each development with the population is a phenomenon. Because there can be many influences on land use development, phenomena can be made of almost anything – from pride in automobiles to expensive petrol and from well-being to exhaust fumes. All these facets have a strong influence on how we will make plans in the future about the land use in our country.

SIGNIFICANT SIDE ISSUES LEAD THE WAY

The second or concept phase of the process of change in **THE MAKING OF** game has the phenomena and ambitions placed on both sides of a matrix at its core. In studying the relationship between ambitions and phenomena, the possibilities for giving direction to the change come to the surface. Exploring the matrix uncovers a new hierarchy in the change. Significant side issues suddenly seem to lead the way and give content to the main issues, while these formerly dominant issues are able to find compromise. This allows culture to direct the change and new identities sprout from the existing ones. It also prevents solving problems first and only then thinking of new identities.

96

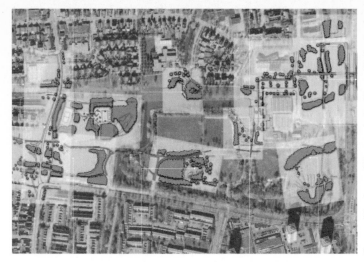

Proposal to change Mheenpark, Apeldoorn, Netherlands.
Illustration: Merijn Groenhart

The end result of the rounds of the game is not a singe
design, or even a single concept. It is a collection of opinions,
thoughts and propositions. The game itself doesn't strive for
consensus. At the end of these rounds, the client and the advisors have a source of information at hand with which to review
the recommendations for the process of change and thereby
actually define the task. The process takes into account the many
concerned and interested parties in its analysis and concept
development, so that the results are recognizable. This analysis
and concept development process actually defines the design
statement. What follows is the actualization of that design statement, the third and planning phase.

This example from Apeldoorn illustrates how the planning
process of **THE MAKING OF** can function.

ACTION-DIRECTING COLOURING PICTURE

In 2002, I became involved in the municipality of Apeldoorn's
plans to renovate the Mheenpark, a park in the Zevenhuizen
neighbourhood. These plans had provoked a real civil upris-
ing. Hundreds of letters of complaint had been submitted, the
council meeting was loudly forced to listen, and an effective
lobby group put in place. A local architect and pedagogue stood
at the head of the democratic resistance movement and succeeded in instigating and keeping a broad protest going. The
municipality's plans also gave them every reason to do so: the
plan presentation sketched a rather negative picture of the park
that the surrounding residents and users did not recognize.
The park was made out to be unsafe and derelict, absolutely
not meeting its supposed purpose and use. The solution was a
large-scale renovation. Reference pictures of sunny and busy
parks from the Mediterranean Sea area were contrasted with
dark photos of the empty Mheenpark on a drizzly autumn Tuesday
afternoon. The possible metamorphosis proposed: with the right
investment, the city of Apeldoorn was ready to give this sombre
park a Mediterranean shine. Even better, thanks to development

along the edges of the park, the money for the changes could be made on location. The plan presentation stressed these edges as the greatest source of evil: they were unusually undefined and messy, therefore a thorn in the eye of urban planners. The action leaders, who lived directly on the edge of the park, mobilized residents to infiltrate into the heart of the action and by forming their own society to give a good stir to the press as well as to use specific campaigns to get at the heart and spirit of park users. All the children from surrounding primary schools thus took home dissident colouring pictures so as to also mobilize their parents.

OPEN PLANNING PROCESS

The protests were successful and the city council rejected the plans for metamorphosis. Because of the upheaval caused by the protest, the city councillor suggested postponing making any new plans for a few years, thinking that the civil anger might cool down and the plans might then be approved. But the formal and informal lobby group that had grown up in the meantime succeeded in forcing renovation plans to be set up immediately and in ensuring that they would have a foremost position on any decisions made. Because the confidence in the town council was not particularly high, an external firm had to take over the planning. We were thus hired with **THE MAKING OF** game. The first hurdle in the project was determining the project plan. Residents wanted to have a decisive influence on every level of detail, while the municipality wanted to leave everything up to the 'open planning' process. Neither was realistic. The council as owner of the land, as the trustee, as the chosen commission and as the body responsible for public order, had much too important a role to avoid defining the objectives such a plan had to fulfil. There was also the risk that once the residents had set up their desired plan that the municipality would still change it with its own agenda and possibilities and thereby take a much too dominant role in the 'open' planning. On the other hand, the residents and users could base their wishes and suggestions on their own experience, but were not qualified in many other aspects. Water usage, vegetation possibilities, and the design and cost of recreational facilities were among the inescapable features of the planning process. In the case of the Mheenpark, we focused the process on constantly joining together skilled expertise with the residents' experience and also on forcing the city to commit to the preconditions of the final result.

The municipality, so mistrusted by the residents, played its role with verve, not by setting a series of cynically inclined clerks against the civil protest but, rather, with its tone of complete disinterest and its lack of organization. The bulk of the associated civil servants kept changing roles or seemed to be hired only temporarily by the city. A number of the employees disappeared in the interim and were replaced during the process, adding another year to the proceedings. As convinced as the residents were of a plot by 'the city' against their situation, the reality was actually much worse. The city seemed to have absolutely no memory or continuity about the whole affair, let alone a plot.

During the rounds of the game that we organized, the residents were not facing their enemy the city, but met one another in a debate. That in itself proved to be a rich source of insights. The protest front was not half as hermetic as had been assumed; rather, it seemed to be a collection of needs and wants that often seemed to conflict with one another. On the other side, the edge of the park did seem to be messy on the map, but absolutely wasn't so in real life. The position of the municipality's designers proved to be the result mainly of these maps and a single visit to the grounds. The confrontation with independent experts and a public check of the proposals with a calculator showed a complete turnaround in the opinion. Suspicion turned into involvement and fear of change into curiosity for the possibilities. Without any more Mediterranean references, an improvement plan was drawn up that was approved not only by the city but also by the residents, and, more importantly, proved achievable. Because the residents had forced the realization of the results of the planning process and the city had made itself as 'open' as possible, the development of the park edges was definitively dropped from the plans. The renovated park opened its doors in 2006.

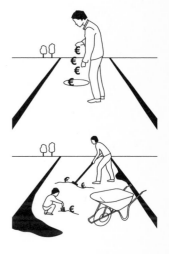

MONEY FOR WATER

In a new residential development, artworks are placed to increase the experiential value once it is built. Art is not the only aspect that forms the experiential value of a residential environment; it takes shape with the combined efforts of all the disciplines involved in spatial planning, such as urban planning, architecture and landscape architecture. In the end, it is also naturally the users of the neighbourhood who, besides experiencing the space, are an integral part of the development of the experiential value of the place. In the **MONEY FOR WATER** proposal, the realization of a lake in a new residential development is the motivation for an art project. The proposal is not to let a landscape architect design the lake ideally and then to let a contractor dig it up so as to open it up to the public at the right moment. The **MONEY FOR WATER** project proposes pumping money into the ground at random, secret locations on the spot of the future lake. During the 'Money for water days', new and old residents each get a plot where they can search for money, meaning that they have to move the soil. This creates a lake which is highly unpredictable and towards which the residents feel a greater attachment.

Proposal for an art application in the new residential development in Elst, 2001

LIFE: THE GAME

Together with Wouter Baars, I developed, for the Art Fort (Dutch: *Kunstfort*) in Haarlemmermeer, **LIFE: THE GAME**. The game, which was played by thirty participants in a space at the Art Fort, simulated the courses of people's lives. The players were divided into four classes and wore their own scoreboards in the form of coloured smocks. The players were confronted with life choices, which could affect their health, knowledge and expertise and degree of wealth and power. They had to present themselves in a talent hunt; they had to find (and perhaps lose) a partner and undergo the rigours of getting through university. The players' scores were ultimately translated into power and hope points. If a player lost all of his/her power or hope, this meant the definitive end of his/her game life. The friends whom the deceased had accumulated in the course of the game could take leave of him/her and equitably distribute his/her accumulated wealth amongst themselves.

The fact that the game irrevocably led to the death of all of the players did not prevent it from generating serious confrontations and much enjoyment and hilarity. Things really got exciting when the best friend of the wealthiest player was kidnapped. Moneybags was not prepared to pay a ransom amounting to half of his wealth, and this in turn cost his friend his life. According to many participants, this was the moment when the game became serious, and became serious for its remainder.

Game of life in the exhibition 'Ruhezeit Abgelaufen', Haarlemmermeer, 2009

In virtually all of my projects, I assign an important role to game playing. In so doing, I use both the game side of seriousness, and the serious side of game playing. In this regard, I included, above in this text, examples of game playing as a 'stimulator of history' (parquetting method) and as a 'developer of useful concepts', and also included an example of the debate method (THE MAKING OF). Provided they are well-played, such games can play a decisive role in concept development and decision making. However, the usefulness of game playing does not stop here. It also possesses special educational properties, as the impulse to want to win in a game ensures that, without even thinking about it, people consistently ensure that they have the requisite skills for attaining the goal of winning. (Recent years have seen the development of a new branch of trade, complete with trade fairs, canvassers, trade unions and trainings around the theme of today's *homo ludens*, or the 'serious gamer'.) The primary task of such 'serious games' is attaining an equilibrium between the goals of 'serious learning' and 'enjoyable play'. Where either of these goals gets the upper hand, the other performs proportionately more poorly, and becomes an impediment.

GUANXI

The principle of learning whilst playing is applicable to virtually all topics and all ages. In China, to be able to do business successfully, one must first have a well-functioning network of contacts. Only then can one produce or trade. Repeatedly, whilst journeying in China, I myself had the opportunity to experience this phenomenon personally. In Mandarin, such a network is called *guanxi*. The GUANXI GAME, which I subsequently developed together with Tanja Reith, enables participants to experience a range of the alternative possibilities one can encounter as an outsider when trying to build up such a network. As a first step, one normally eats a good meal with new contacts. Before you know it, you are singing karaoke with them. In turn, you meet a friend of a friend, visit a temple or are even invited to a mysterious guanxi club. One's success is, however, not just determined

AS-IF

GUANXI GAME
关系

Situation
You want to do business in China. In order to do that succesfully you need a good network of contacts (that is called Guanxi in Chinese).

With the Guanxi game you learn all about building networks in China. Learn how to build up and recognize all the Guanxi you need!

Board for Guanxi Game.
Design: Annemarie van den Berg

by good relations, strategy and politics – chance, luck and negative experiences also play important roles. Not knowing how important hierarchy is in a Chinese company, not being able to eat with chopsticks or not knowing that, contrary to expectation, *you* yourself have to pay the female escort in the karaoke bar even if the host has ordered her, can be disastrous to one's network. In this two-hour-long board game, one learns about the different things that can be encountered on the path to creating a network in China, how to deal with them, profit from them or avoid their negative effects, respectively.

BULB

The website, www.bulb-web.nl, enables pupils in the Dune and Bulb Region to discover the past, present and future of their region. The website contains a treasure-trove of information, packaged in maps, informative items, cartoons, games, photos, film fragments and assignments. BULB is an interdisciplinary website that can be used in connection with the subjects, geography, history, social studies and cultural studies. The website's educational content is based on the material and immaterial finds, facts, ideas and designs which resulted from the project SOUL AND SOIL, adapted/rewritten for BULB, and which consists, amongst other things, of short texts, photos, film fragments, drawings and cartoons. The aim of BULB is to make pupils conscious of the history of their own region and to enable them to see that it will be possible to do things with it in future (see further pp 196-207).

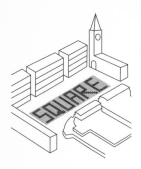

SQUARESAVER

The **SQUARESAVER** is a variant of the screensaver, from the world of the computer. The original function of screensavers was to prevent text from being burnt into displays by means of an animation which ensured that there was an image on the screen that remained in motion. The early nineties saw the development of a specific culture around the phenomenon of the screensaver. Hundreds of possibilities appeared on the market. These included having one's screen image at turns eaten up and converted into a dog's kennel, or having it produce fireworks shows and the like. Screensavers have long lost their original function, as today's generation of computer displays is no longer susceptible to burn-in. Despite this, the number of screensavers available continues to grow, and it is now even possible for computer users to create screensavers using their own images, thus driving those little frames with family photos off desks and onto computer screens.

The screensaver gives computers a meaning at moments when they are not in use, enabling them to form fully fledged parts of their surroundings. Analogously, the **SQUARESAVER** plays this same role for Anton de Kom Square in Amsterdam-Zuidoost, appearing at those times when the square is not in use for an outdoor market. The **SQUARESAVER** consists of a system of transparent blocks, based on a two-metre grid, mounted in the square's pavement. The blocks contain LEDs capable of producing any colour. The blocks can be driven remotely by means of specially written programmes and a central computer. The **SQUARESAVER** ensures that the square remains in motion and does not 'burn-in'.

Proposal for an artistic use of the public space at Anton de Kom Square, Amsterdam, 2003

Stills from **BULB** website. Design: Antenna-Men

WATER GARDEN

The UNESCO world heritage site, the Beemster, also turned out to be a source of inspiration for a game. Despite its UNESCO status, the things that make the Beemster so special are not directly apparent to those visiting the site for the first time. For instance, one neither sees the unending series of windmills that reclaimed the area, nor a characteristic pumping station. What is special about the Beemster can, namely, be found in its totality: from great (the entire polder) to small (the farmstead with its buildings, fences, bridges and plantings), the Beemster forms one single coherent whole. The history of the Beemster, which, like that of a third of the Netherlands, is based on laying a ring dike and, in turn, permanently removing the water in the ground by means of pump machines, is, for many a visitor to this country, entirely unimaginable.

Enabling the visitor to imagine this should form the start of any successful visit to the Beemster. This can be done by means of the Water Garden. The heart of this garden is formed by a model of the entire Beemster at a scale of 1:500. The model consists of a 'pit' measuring 26 by 16 metres in the characteristic shape of the Beemster, surrounded by a ring dike. The ditches also contain real water. The water system is connected to the more highly elevated ring canal, dug around the model. At the spots where windmills originally stood for the purpose of pumping the water out of the polder, different types of pump have been installed in the water garden. All of the pumps require human effort to function, and include: a classic hand-pump, a seesaw, as well as fitness equipment. By operating the pumps, visitors help to reclaim the polder, and in turn to allow the characteristic Beemster pattern to emerge. A scoreboard indicates the volume of water displaced and the capacity of the pumps. In this way, visitors not familiar with reclamation, impoldering and living below sea level are provided with an unforgettable experience. At a stroke, they gain insight into the essence of the Beemster. Upon emerging from the visitors' centre after having drunk coffee, they will see that the polder once again is fully inundated.

104

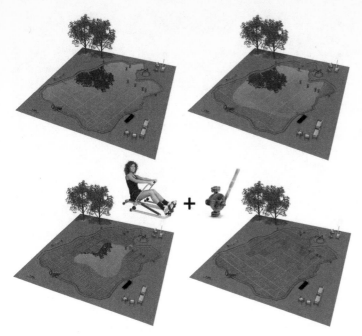

Proposal for a water garden for the Beemster, Netherlands.
Illustrations: Olivier Scheffer

ARTIFICIAL GRASS: ALWAYS GREEN
AND LOW-MAINTENANCE

Even traditional play areas for children can provide an occasion for learning something. One can, for example, re-use a play area's existing qualities whilst not having to confine oneself to just referring to it. For an area in Hilversum originally designed by Willem Dudok in the 1930s that was being renovated by architect Hans Ruijssenaars, I proposed a playground.

Dudok, who from 1927 until 1954, was city architect for the municipality of Hilversum, left a very clear mark on the city's appearance. Ruijssenaars' plan ensured that the area would become even more Dudokesque than it had been. The result was spectacular, such that it is impossible to distinguish between Dudok 1.0 and 2.0. In draughting his master plan, Ruijssenaars had studied historical photos of the district in great detail and observed that the public space was unusually empty. Even though in the early 1930s, when these photos had been made, virtually no one had an automobile, there were hardly any public amenities/facilities, and the site's greenery had only just been planted, this did not stop Ruijssenaars from wanting to restore the 'original' situation down to the last detail. Shrubs were removed, limits were placed on parking, and the playground that had existed in the middle of the green area of Van 't Hoff Square also removed. This was the situation when I was commissioned to devise proposals for how art and culture could be deployed in this environment. As Ruijssenaars' plans were already being implemented at the time, and it was too late for a significant intervention in the planning for the area, my first proposal was a cosmetic one. To guarantee the desired appearance for the square in both summer and winter – and even under the worst possible drought conditions –,

105

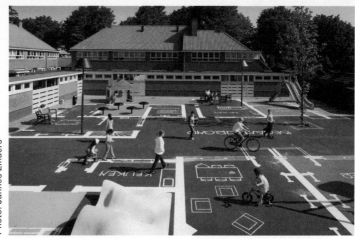

Playground on 't Hoffstraat, Hilversum, Netherlands.
Photo: Jannes Linders

I proposed to make the grass cover of Van 't Hoff Square of synthetic grass: always green and low-maintenance. (By way of an ironic reference to the black-and-white photos which had served as the basis for Ruijssenaars' plans, a somewhat grey-ish synthetic grass cover could even be opted for!) To my great surprise, though, the Municipality of Hilversum informed me that experience had taught them that a synthetic grass cover requires more maintenance than real grass. As a result, this proposal did not get off the ground. My second proposal, one for a playground in the inner court, did manage to get through.

AS-IF INTERIORS, AS-IF DWELLINGS

Ruijssenaars recognized and respected the existing qualities of Dudok's dwellings, but, to meet present-day needs, nevertheless introduced modifications, the most prominent of which being those he made to their floor plans. As a way of showing how these dwellings looked in Dudok's day, I proposed incorporating floor plans by Dudok in my design for the above-mentioned playground.

When the floor plans, taken from Dudok's original drawings at a scale of 1:1, are plotted on the inner court, the first thing one notices is how small these original dwellings were. The living room, kitchen and bedroom are all immediately recognizable. Naturally, the playground equipment takes complete advantage of the floor plans: the bench and lamps are in the living room, the refuse bin in the kitchen, the shack in the garden; the swing hangs between the sliding doors and the slide begins in the staircase. The legally required soft floors around the equipment were easy to integrate. The original floor plans clearly offer play opportunities and directly evoke something of the architecture of Dudok in its original surroundings, but without cultural-heritage references. Thus, the playground constitutes a kind of **DUDOK FOR BEGINNERS**. It re-uses a typical Dudok quality in an entirely foreign context.

The playground is only accessible in the daytime to parents accompanied by children through the age of eight. The terrain is closed off on all sides and only accessible via a gate, whose design is based on one of the most beautiful gates ever

Entrance railing to the playground.
Photo: Jannes Linders

designed by Dudok, that for the Noorderbegraafplaats cemetery in Hilversum. The gate bears the text: 'AS THOUGH DOING-AS-IF WERE NOT ALSO SIMPLY DOING' ('ALSOF DOEN ALSOF NIET OOK GEWOON DOEN IS'), which one sees upon leaving the playground. After the children have enjoyed themselves in the as-if interiors of the as-if dwellings, this text has an extraordinarily comforting effect on the young reader, for, in 'doing-as-if', children train their ability to function in the grown-up world. For grown-ups, it should have more the character of a warning, as they are not leaving the 'do-as-if' world, but are re-entering the very surroundings in which 'doing-as-if' (e.g., building in a historicizing manner) has now become extraordinarily ordinary (see further pp 184-195).

THE GAME SIDE OF SERIOUSNESS, THE SERIOUS SIDE OF GAME PLAYING

A good game has no fixed form, no fixed medium and no fixed location. It adapts itself to the given situation, location and players.

Game playing and seriousness in no way exclude one another. Game playing forms part of the most serious of processes, and no form of game playing is that far removed from seriousness. Where game playing and seriousness do become separated, the openness of outlook and the curiosity that are so essential to the cultural character of spatial planning, disappear from the picture. The pleasure borne of the confluence of game playing and seriousness contains the kernel of every process of change. Game playing has the potential to provide us with insight into processes of change, insight that far transcends our own interests or perceptions. Game playing enables us, for a moment, to stand in the shoes of the relevant alderman, or even conceive our own concept for the process of change in question – after all, the best ideas are always the ones we think of ourselves.

THE CONCEPT

In the preceding chapters I have demonstrated the importance of designing the process of change itself as opposed to making comforting final images. I have explained the importance of naming phenomena and goals of transforming existing qualities in new contexts. And with that, I have shown how you can turn current problems into future icons. But even the best intentions depend on whoever implements them and the position occupied by that person. The position of 'game leader in the field of change' is still omitted on the budget estimates of the bodies responsible. Expertise in content is generally linked to one of the sectors concerned. Urban design supervisors, city architects, sociological researchers and cultural-historical advisors are appointed in processes overseen and controlled by project management agencies. This separation of content and organization threatens to eliminate intuition from the process of change. And intuition is precisely what is needed to break open processes and reveal surprising connections. A task to be performed by the concept manager.

TICKING OFF CULTURE

The concept manager connects the process with the content and translates the results of the research in the assignment. Even during the most conscientiously conducted, content-rich process those connections do not appear of their own accord, and the decision moments in a process cannot always be predicted. Unexpected turns and opportunities to link content to preconditions directly can crop up at any moment. It is the job of the concept manager to be present and to recognize these opportunities. The concept manager is responsible for both the quality of the content and the smooth progress of the planning process. For a *homo universalis*, a specialist in many areas of science to art and management, the world has become far too complicated. The concept manager specializes in the relationships and defines the transitional moments between the different phases of research, concept development and planning without being tied to any particular one of the disciplines involved. Moreover, he is fed by the client, informants and testers.

DYSCARTOLEXIA

Satellite navigation equipment is no longer exclusive equipment; it's become standard in even the cheapest cellphones. At the same time, we see the drawbacks of the satellite navigation generation growing. Almost every day you hear about motorists who faithfully follow the instructions of that reassuring voice in the car and, as a result, drive into oncoming traffic, end up in a ditch, or try to take motorway exits that don't even exist. Just a question of time before we have the first court case against a satellite navigator who wrote off his car by listening and not looking. To prevent all such court cases, major roadworks on the motorway are now accompanied by warnings to switch off the navigation system, and to do it quickly. Our loss of ability to read our surroundings will be a big handicap in the twenty-first century. Very soon the inability to filter non-linguistic information from our surroundings (dyspictolexia), and the inability to read maps (dyscartolexia), will become common new diseases and cost the national health system a lot of money. To prevent this, we must insist on our right to get lost.

Observation, 2007

MANAGER

The concept manager.

From a distance, the difference between a concept manager and a process manager probably doesn't seem so big. In processes headed by a concept manager, he is also responsible for a clear procedure, the involvement of all parties, and the pursuit of a good outcome. But the criteria for a good outcome are different for a concept manager than for a manager whose focus is limited to the process itself. The concept manager strives, first and foremost, for a recognizable level of spatial continuity and ensures that existing qualities play a concrete role in the process of change, even if that is not so evident. For the concept manager, culture is not just another item on a checklist that needs to be ticked off; rather, it has the potential to lend direction and guidance to the whole process. To reach consensus, the concept manager searches for a new hierarchy of content instead of a fragmented administrative hierarchy. In that, he does not focus solely on the final result, but on the process and how it is shaped. From that perspective he also works on how the process is structured and develops new tools. The result can be just about anything: a book, a game, a research project, an artwork, an exhibition, or a spatial design.

PLAN MASTER

The concept manager dons a variety of hats during the process. First of all he formulates the assignment; he specifies the commission that stems from the concept phase. The question is not only how that strong concept can be specified but also how it can develop and be adjusted over time. After all, not a single landscape is stable and predictable. New developments are occurring all the time, not only physically but also in terms of legislation, that cast another light on plans drawn up earlier. A good concept is therefore not an inflexible master plan with X's on the map and accompanied by hermetic argumentation about the location and intended nature of those X's. A good concept moves with developments and contains a strategy of presence. In the process, emphasis is put on those who can undertake to make adaptations all the time. This is the personified master plan, of rather the *plan master*, who is positioned to constantly 'formulate' the content of the assignment on the basis of information and discussions and then selects those involved and oversees the subsequent implementation.

By no means does the process of change end while a good plan is being formulated. New insights, altered political, economic and social conditions, incidents, and chance all influence the situation during the remaining period of implementation. For the concept manager, too, involvement therefore doesn't end once a good plan has been formulated. After the design of the process of change itself, its conclusion and identity, the resulting design of the assignment and the supervision of the (spatial) plan, the concept manager finally designs his further involvement in the proceedings.

Determining the qualities of the change is where the power of the concept manager lies. Unimpeded by any confined sector position or a fixed final image, he charts the qualities and allows them to exert an influence in the field of change. This forms the core of the culture of spatial planning. And although it is not my intention to argue in favour of the appointment of a concept manager in every process of change, a preliminary investigation based on the cultural dimension of the situation can make the result more than the sum of the sectors involved. That does demand a well-developed curiosity about a whole host of issues that shape the built environment and their effects. But above all, it requires pleasure in playing and seriousness in organizing space under the guidance of a game master of the Game Urbanism.

ESSENTIAL MARGIN

In April 2007 forty problem neighbourhoods in the Netherlands were selected on account of their urgent need to be 'tackled'. This neighbourhood operation is of an unprecedented scale and complexity. Both the physical and social aspects of the neighbourhoods need to be improved vigorously. Strengthening of the identity and marketing are important aspects in the process. To put a better complexion on the neighbourhoods, strange connections are sometimes made between the current situation and the desired character, while vital opportunities in the margins are often left unexploited. Moreover, such plans are generally aimed at the desired end result and pay little attention to the so-called intervening period between the start of transformation and its completion. This period can be as long as fifteen or even twenty years, long enough for a whole generation to grow up. The Interval Development Company (IDC) model was therefore developed to ensure that opportunities in the margins can be exploited and to strip the neighbourhood improvement process of rigid thinking in final images.

Proposal within the framework of the
Laboratory of the Interval,
The Hague, 2008

WORKBOOK

PARQUETTE
PP 116 – 135

DES BEEMSTERS
PP 136 – 151

PARQUETTE

PARQUETTE

OUTLINE DESIGN

Devised in 1991 by Hans Venhuizen, **PARQUETTING** (derived from, *parquette*, an amalgam of *parquet* and *maquette*, the French for *architectural model*) is a method for involving the factors of time and chance, in the planning of new urban areas. Parquetting deploys the fishbone structure as a reorganizing principle. Employing simulation in the form of a game, the **PARQUETTING METHOD** reveals the positive side of conflict in urban-planning processes. Such a simulation game is not intended to yield a definitive design for a desired urban situation, but rather, an outline design. The outline design makes the relevant location unique: in it, obstacles to, and limitations upon, a context-free, ideal plan emerge. A credible history of the location, an actual or imagined vacant terrain, becomes visible. And it is the very imperfection of the situation at hand that makes the design process that is now to commence special. The wishes and future plans of residents, administrators and property developers are projected onto the outline design. This in turn forces the planners to take careful account of its contents: they must respect its various settlements and include its lines of development in their plans. **PARQUETTING** employs the herringbone pattern as a principle of reorganization.

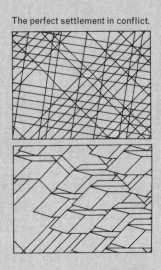

The perfect settlement in conflict.

game, an architectural model is left of an imperfect ideal: a district consisting of fragments of missed ideals – mixed up, kooky and damaged, but each in and of itself strong enough to survive. The architectural models that have resulted from the game are in turn sawn into strips of a size comparable to a half-neighbourhood in the ideal settlement. Finally, as a final stroke of fate, the fragments are rearranged, in an entirely random manner, to form a new whole, featuring a herringbone pattern. The **PARQUETTE** resulting from the **PARQUETTING METHOD** is a starting point for further development.

capacity in order to be able to start building there. Located in the Flevo Polder, Almere is a 'new town', which since its establishment less than thirty years ago has managed to become the Netherlands' fifth-largest city. There is still so much undeveloped space in Almere that new residential districts can be realized beside one another without any difficulty. Such new districts are designed entirely in accordance with the ambitions and possibilities of the respective times in which they are put up. The substrate on which these districts are built has few limitations, in contrast to what is frequently the case with 'old land'. There are no pre-existing structures or examples of special 'old nature' to stand in the way – actually a pity, as it is just this kind of confrontation with limitations that can increase the uniqueness of such districts. In contrast, the **PARQUETTING METHOD** makes it possible for history to take place before the design process begins, enabling the settlement to be built to have individualizing limitations imposed upon it. Through a game pitting the Dwelling Consumers against the Pioneers, fragments of new settlements can come into being in the Coastal zone which will in turn be the best bits in the future urban fabric. As an 'ultimate act' in making this area one's own, the architectural model is then sawn into pieces and rearranged as a herringbone parquet floor, so that one can feel entirely at home here, even on an urban scale.

Herringbone paving in ancient Rome, Italy. Source: www.wikipedia.org, Trajan's Market

Exhibition floor plan, **PARQUETTE** Coastal zone, Almere, Netherlands.

PARQUETTE SETTLEMENT GAME

The **PARQUETTE SETTLEMENT GAME** involves a minimum of two parties. Each party has the same objective: realizing *its* ideal settlement at the up to now context-free location. The ideal settlement is, by definition, a simplification. This was represented in ideal form in the first **PARQUETTE** with a collection of houses, arranged in such a manner that the occupants of each respective house are at a readable distance from, and thus has a clearly defined relationship with respect to their neighbours, their street, their neighbourhood and, finally, their urban district.

HERRINGBONE PATTERN

The herringbone pattern is an amazing cultural constant, found in, amongst other things, pottery, textiles, interiors and pavement. The herringbone pattern was already employed by the Romans in brick houses, often as a decorative border. In later architectural styles, it frequently fulfils more than an ornamental function, with the bricks of an entire facade being laid in herringbone fashion, presumably because the long, narrow bricks could be employed more efficiently in this manner than when laid horizontally. This efficiency also explains why, since some thirty years, when the streets of historic city centres are renewed in an authentic manner, their cast stones and concrete paving blocks are laid in a herringbone pattern. This system of organization is incredibly robust: it easily withstands modern motorcar and lorry traffic due to that fact that the 'braided' stones always stay in place. In addition, such a street continues to be beautiful and has an extremely 'homey' look, which would also explain why parquet floors have been laid using the pattern for more than 250 years.

ALMERE

In 2008, **PARQUETTING** was applied to the Coastal zone in Almere, at the time an area waiting to be developed, which explains why the 'planning machines' were running at top

The perfect settlement.

The projections of the respective parties concerning the ideal residential district all differ slightly from one another, such that each party's ideal settlement stands in the way of that of the other(s). By means of the game's rules, different forms of conflict and unexpected development are simulated. At the end of the

Image on previous page: **PARQUETTE** in Museum De Paviljoens in Almere, Netherlands, 2008. Photo: Gert Jan van Rooij

PARQUETTE

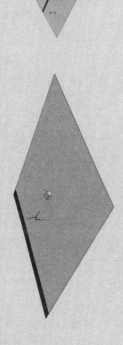

GAME 1: PARQUETTE

Participants

– The Pioneers: have the romantic ideal of living self-sufficiently. To be able to live self-sufficiently, the Pioneers need a parcel measuring 135 x 135 m.

– The Dwelling Consumers: choose their own residential and living environment from a range of possible residential types offered to them by the market. They need a variety of residential types, so that their various wishes can be catered to.

Board game about competing ideal plans.

PARQUETTE

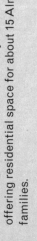

In the settlement game, all players try to realize their ideal settlement on the same site.

Playing the game

All parties have rolled out their ideal maps of the Coastal zone and make fierce attempts to realize their ideal settlements upon it. They compete with one another and encounter limitations in terms of space, the natural environment and the regulations in force. As a result of these limitations, it will not be possible for both parties to realize their ideals. The architectural model that results is a chaos of fragments from the two contrasting settlements. These fragments are nevertheless robust enough to remain intact, but they have undergone too much damage to be able entirely to determine future developments. The model (scale 1:250) is then sawn into blocks and rearranged as a parquet floor. The size of the resulting **PARQUETTE** is half that of an average Almere street, namely 25 x 100 m, offering residential space for about 15 Almere families.

Game result

The game does not result in a definitive design for a desired urban situation, but rather, a design presenting an outline design. The outline design makes the relevant location unique: obstacles and limitations have been added and a credible history of the location has become visible. And it is the very imperfection of the situation at hand that makes the design process which is now to commence special. The wishes and plans for the future of residents, administrators and property developers are projected onto the outline design. This in turn forces the planners to take careful account of its contents: they must respect its various settlements and include its lines of development in their plans, as opposed to drawing up a context-free, ideal plan.

The result of the settlement game is cut into pieces and arranged randomly in a herringbone pattern.

An outline design for the Coastal zone in Almere, Netherlands. Photo: Gert Jan van Rooij

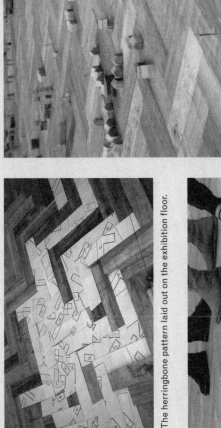

The herringbone pattern laid out on the exhibition floor.

Various houses, apartments and pioneers' homes are built. Photo: Gert Jan van Rooij

COASTAL ZONE

FOREST ZONE

PRESENT
RESIDENTS

PARQUETTE

new Builders and Administrators start again at zero. Residents cannot resign, regardless of how dissatisfied they are with the result. Following each round, a number of the New Residents relocate to the Present Residents, since they will now be commencing residence in the new residential district. Some of the Present Residents look for new accommodation and, as a result, become New Residents. The second and third phases go as did the first, except that there is less time available for consultation. The parties continue to build upon their existing state of trust/satisfaction/profit, unless they have been replaced.

When the game has ended, the score is determined and a record of the course of the game drawn up. What has transpired? How much 'programme' has been realized? How is the result to be characterized? Have the Administrators been able to retain the trust of the present Residents? Have the Builders made a profit and are the New Residents satisfied? Can we realize the settlement in this manner?

Filling out the form of choices.
Photo: Museum De Paviljoens

Situation in game of **URBANISTS** in Museum De Paviljoens Almere, Netherlands.

GAME 2: URBANISTS

The simulation game **URBANISTS** determines how the desired number of dwellings can be built in the new settlement.

Participants

– The Administrators (three persons) represent the municipal government. They bear

task to realize 1500 dwellings in three phases. Each party is provided with an explanation regarding the choices to be made, based on its profile. Although the relevant choices and formulations are identical, their profiles will differ significantly from one another. The interests of Present Residents are different from those of New Residents, and those of Residents are different from those of Builders. The information

A trial settlement is built.
Photo: Museum De Paviljoens

Officials steer the building process.
Photo: Museum De Paviljoens

responsibility for future developments in the area, and ultimately decide on how the Coastal zone will be developed.

–The Builders (three persons) would like to build dwellings in Almere. By building houses, they can earn profits, which is an important objective for them.

–The Present Residents (making up one-third of the other persons) already live in the area and it is because of the **PARQUETTE SETTLEMENT GAME** that they are attending. They are sceptical about the new developments in their area and hope that these will not be detrimental to it.

–It is the wish of the Future Residents (the rest of the other persons) to live in Almere in the future. They clearly have wishes concerning how they want to live in their future houses, and hope that these will be accommodated to the greatest extent possible.

Playing the game

The area being planned is to be developed In three phases (see ill. pp 126-127). One planning phase will be developed in each round of the game.

At the start of each round, the participants fill in an option form with four questions relating to the spatial elaboration of the area (see pp 130-131).

Choices must be made as to the type of expansion, and the type, density and location of the houses that are to result. The Administrators also consider the available possibilities and draw up a preliminary programme. It is their

sheet explains what the different choices will mean for each party.

The Administrators consider the programme, the spatial effects that will result from realization and how satisfied the different parties will be. All of the forms are submitted to the Administrators, who in turn produce their proposal. At the same time, the three other parties start building a test settlement in accordance with their ideal.

The Administrators present their plan to the other parties, leaving time for a short discussion (consultation round). If needed, the Administrators can then adjust their plans in response to comments from the other parties. Three minutes later, they present the choices that will be made concerning the different questions by placing representations of these on the scoreboard. Then, in accordance with the Administrators' plan, everyone can start building houses, whilst receiving instructions from the Builders and, possibly, corrections from the Administrators.

Then, a score is determined as to the extent to which the three parties' wishes (profit/satisfaction/trust) correspond to the plan that has been executed. If the Builders end with a negative score, they will go bankrupt and will be replaced with participants from another party. The same applies to the Administrators. If too little of what they have done has been in accordance with the wishes of the other parties, such that they have ended with a negative score, they resign and are replaced. The

Game result

Following a number of rounds, participants have gained more insight into the dynamics of urban development and the different positions which can be identified within the context of these dynamics. At the same time, a catalogue of special planning possibilities for the area has been compiled (see pp 132-133).

129

Image on previous page: Laid out for the game of **URBANISTS. PARQUETTE** in Museum De Paviljoens in Almere, Netherlands, 2008. Photo: Gert Jan van Rooij

PARQUETTE

Type of expansion

Type of development

New neighbourhood nearby

Overlapping

Organic expansion

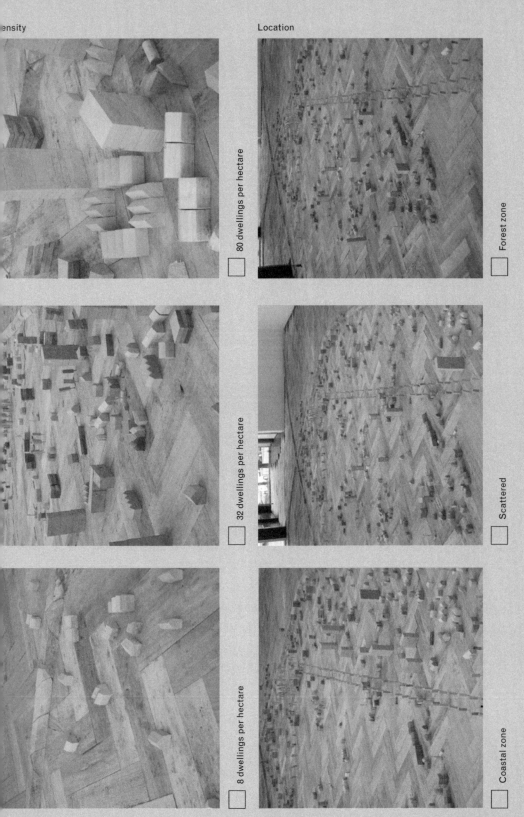

80 dwellings per hectare

32 dwellings per hectare

8 dwellings per hectare

Forest zone

Scattered

Coastal zone

Form on which participants can indicate their preferences for future developments.

131

PARQUETTE

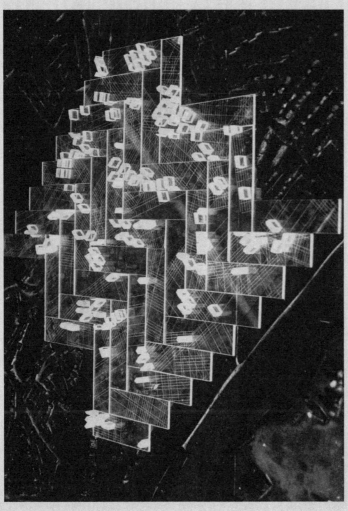

Glazed **PARQUETTE SETTLEMENT** in Arnhem, Netherlands, 1991.

BACKGROUND

The first **PARQUETTE SETTLEMENT** was created in 1991 as a wooden landscape, in which not only (floor)plans but landscape qualities were simulated (see p. 69). In the same year, the same Parquette Settlement was produced in a glass variant, as a hopeful metaphor for the resurrection of a destroyed city.

PARQUETTING also turned out highly useful for planning at the regional scale. In 1996, Hans Venhuizen carried out, for the West-Brabant region, a study into the possibilities for as-signing to the herringbone organizational principle the leading role in dealing with the many developments which the region faced. In 2000, the parquet organizational principle was applied to a garden at *Amarant*, Tilburg's institution for the intellectually handicapped. Here, the **PARQUET GARDEN** was realized: a garden measuring 3300 m2, specially designed as a sense-stimulating environment for individu-als with an intellectual handicap. The garden consisted of about 85 'chambers' measuring 3 x 7.5 m. Each chamber provided only *one* experience, in which the visitor could feel entirely enveloped. The chambers were ar-ranged in a herringbone pattern, so that, when viewed from the air, they gave the impression of an immense parquet floor: the **PARQUET GARDEN**. The herringbone organizational principle employed made the garden flexible: not only could the content of each chamber be changed as desired but, in addition, the

132

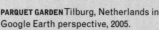

PARQUET GARDEN Tilburg, Netherlands in Google Earth perspective, 2005.

Model for **PARQUET GARDEN** Tilburg, Netherlands, 2000. Photo: Paul Dekker

Version based on historical plan of Breda, 1990.

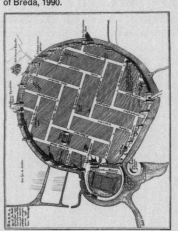

Herringbone pattern for West-Brabant, Netherlands, 1996.

Acknowledgements
PARQUETTE and **URBANISTS** were set up from October 2008 to March 2009 during the exhibition 'Teamwork' in Museum de Paviljoens Almere.
A project by Hans Venhuizen, with Mark van der Wegen, Brigitta van Weeren, Erik-Jan Mans, Els Brouwer and Annemarie van den Berg.
At the invitation of Museum de Paviljoens: Macha Roesink, Annick Kleizen, Irina Leifer and Mireille de Putter.

principle yielded a wide choice of irregular chamber sizes and shapes at the edges of the terrain. The arrangement of the garden could be changed whenever desired, without the garden's usefulness or concept being lost. Experiences were structured to extend over several chambers. Various elements of these experiences, such as the bridges in the pond or the drain pipes in earthen taluds, were also governed by the herringbone principle. What ultimately resulted was a garden offering a multitude of experiences, in which it was a pleasure to wander, without the need to lose one's way. In 2009, expansion of the grounds of Amarant led to the garden's disappearance.

The concept of the herringbone organization was prompted by Hans Venhuizen's 1990 adaptation of the medieval town plan of his birthplace Breda. The new composition of streets and functions resulted in a convincing image, which even incited a yearning for the imaginary historical situation.

133

Image on next page: Result of the game of **URBANISTS** game on the **PARQUETTE SETTLEMENT** in Museum De Paviljoens, Almere, Netherlands.

DES BEEEMSTERS

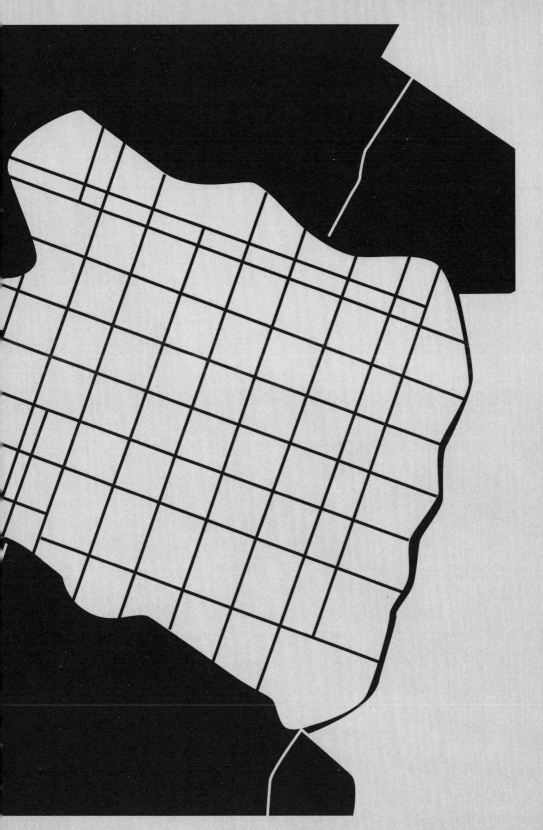

DES BEEMSTERS

CULTURAL HERITAGE AS INTERMEDIARY

In 2005, employing the 'brand name' DES BEEMSTERS (Dutch for 'typical of the Beemster', an old fashioned and short way of stating what is typical for this area), an ad-hoc combination brought together by Hans Venhuizen and comprised of Bureau Venhuizen, Steenhuis stedenbouw/landschap and REDscape Landscape and Urbanism, drew up a development vision for the Beemster district under the aspect of its status as UNESCO World Heritage Site. The idea of the initiative was not to present a map of historic sites for the purpose of protecting existing cultural heritage, but rather, a strategy in which cultural heritage functions as an intermediary in approaching spatial planning issues. Des Beemsters in turn expanded into an approach for actively and constructively involving (cultural-heritage) qualities in the current spatial planning discussions around land reclamation, and resulted in an organizational model for the integral treatment of these issues.

In addition to designing the process and 'identity', Des Beemsters, Bureau Venhuizen bore responsibility for distilling out ambitions and phenomena from the relevant data compiled, moderating THE MAKING OF and designating projects from it which would promote the process of change in the polder

THE MAKING OF DES BEEMSTERS

DES BEEMSTERS commenced in the spring of 2005 with the gathering of information of a broad nature concerning land reclamation and its history, current culture and politics, as well as any other aspects which influence, or could influence, spatial developments in the polder. Des Beemsters staff visited archives and consulted with their administrators, studied the landscape and also interviewed a heterogeneous selection of spokespersons, ranging from farmers and other entrepreneurs, to priests, journalists and organizers of local events. The team consulted numerous reports and other policy documents from various sectors, political groupings, governments, lobby clubs and interested/affected parties, presenting various interpretations of the Beemster's qualities, many of which turned out difficult to harmonize with one another. The study yielded, amongst other things, the ingredients

Three rounds of the game THE MAKING OF, in which some 35 interested/affected parties from the Beemster took part, yielded twenty proposals involving combinations of phenomena and ambitions. In addition, detailed investigation was devoted to two specific tasks: developing the farmsteads and creating more water storage facilities. Together, the proposals and the commentary on these from the debate, combined with the results of the study, resulted in the report *Des Beemsters I*, a development vision for the Beemster, based on its intrinsic qualities.

DES BEEMSTERS I AND II

Following its approval by the municipal council in 2006, the report *Des Beemsters I* underwent further elaboration. The development vision for *Des Beemsters II* was worked out in the form of twelve concrete projects concerning, amongst other things, water, farmsteads, residential architecture, and the effects of horse breeding on the landscape. The projects assessed the previously drawn up game rules, which were then translated into municipal policy. Portions of the projects dovetailed directly with the Rural Area Zoning Plan soon to be drawn up. Three other projects, which added to existing knowledge about specific developments in the Beemster would serve as a basis for adjustments to municipal policy. A third group of projects concerned two concrete architectural tasks with both a rural and an international character.

THE MAKING OF in the Beemster, Netherlands. Photo: Dieuwertje Komen

DES BEEMSTERS logo

whilst safeguarding its intrinsic qualities. We also designed the Bureau Des Beemsters and instigated the creation of the Quality Team, comprised of experts and entrusted with advising the municipality on the quality of the spatial plans to be implemented. Hans Venhuizen remained involved in the further realization of six relevant projects.

– in other words the requisite ambitions and phenomena – for the game, **THE MAKING OF**. The ambitions included, amongst others, providing more water storage facilities, making infrastructural improvements and bringing change to farmsteads. As phenomena, we identified, amongst other things, the meaning of solidarity, world heritage, and isolation as an opportunity.

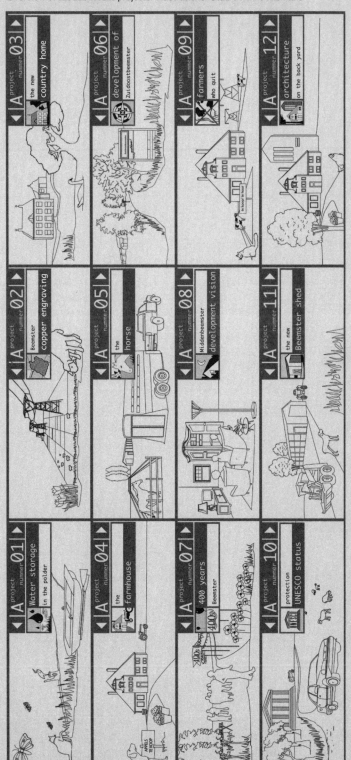

141

Image on previous page: De Beemster from the ring dike. Photo: Dieuwertje Komen

DES BEEMSTERS

143

DES BEEMSTERS

BUREAU DES BEEMSTERS

To execute the projects and anchor the working method opted for in the Beemster itself, a special organization was created: Bureau Des Beemsters. Headed by a concept manager and facilitated by the municipality, the bureau identifies and inventories the polder's qualities, both physical and social, and takes steps to preserve them through development. The bureau coordinates the elaboration of projects, but also 'feeds' the planning process by organizing lectures, debates, workshops, competitions and exhibitions. It is also responsible for bringing the different parties together and raising the requisite funds.

Bureau Des Beemsters was deliberately not located within the municipal Department of Spatial Planning, or that of culture, but rather, within the Municipal Directorate for General Management, from which position it is able to direct the changing and diverse teams of municipal personnel and external experts from both the Department of Spatial Planning and the Department of Culture. The bureau's location also enables it to give equal amounts of attention to the physical and cultural sides of spatial planning. The bureau's activities include both assessing spatial planning for cultural-heritage-related qualities and clearly identifying these. This enables it to focus attention continually on the role played by the Beemster's intrinsic qualities and to define this role in terms of the tasks at hand. Bureau

Des Beemsters was established in 2007 and will cease to exist in 2012, when the polder will have existed for exactly 400 years, and by which time the spatial updating of the spatial actualization of the polder for the present generation will have been brought to completion. Until that time, the term **DES BEEMSTERS** will ensure an integral approach to the spatial planning tasks of land reclamation, in which the cultural-heritage-related qualities of the Beemster will function as intermediary.

Bureau Des Beemsters has initiated a range of studies and projects in which identifying the current value of cultural heritage was the focus of attention. Below, three of these – copper engraving, farmstead makers and water management – are described briefly.

COPPER ENGRAVING

Water unmistakably forms one of the prime components of the Beemster's identity. Widely regarded as Des Beemsters, the original ditch pattern from 1612 must, in the view of all interested/affected parties, be preserved. The copper engraving from 1644 in which this pattern is laid down, is one of the most detailed of all historic representations in map form of the Beemster, and is frequently cited as a point of reference in discussions concerning the heart of the Beemster (see pp 142-143). The perception is widespread that what was laid down in this plan is sacrosanct, with an almost mythical significance being imputed

to this copper engraving. This is surely due to the fact that, until now, no one has ever drawn a comparison between the historic plot plan and the current situation. In 2008, at the initiative of **DES BEEMSTERS**, such a comparison was undertaken. A historical representation of the Beemster dating from 1658, identical to that in the copper engraving, was appropriately adapted and added, as a layer, to the Large-Scale Standard Map of the Netherlands (GBKN), such that all changes made to the water system in the past 400 years were now also visible on the map.

Organisational diagram of Bureau Des Beemsters and its surroundings. Design: Studio Minke Themans

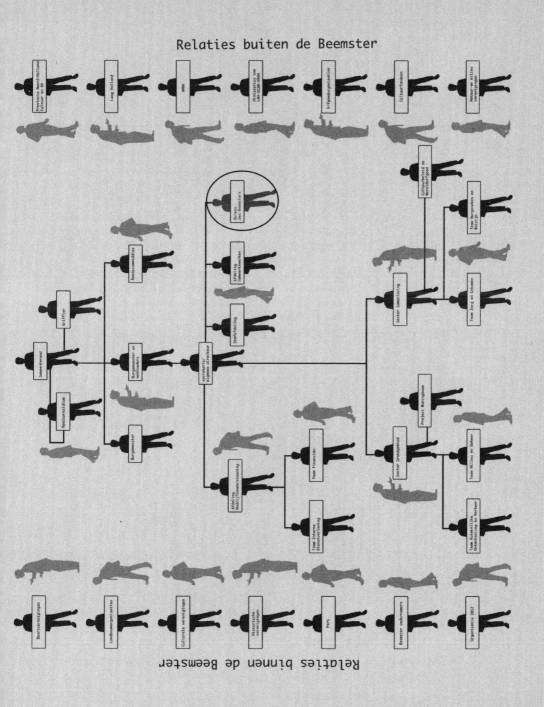

Map of land reclamation in the Beemster, Netherlands. This map shows the water level relative to ground level and indicates where the ground is too wet. Illustration: Hoogheemraadschap Hollands Noorderkwartier/Maarten Poort

DES BEEMSTERS

Legenda
Partikuliere bemalingen
Drooglegging
1,7 - >
1,6 - 1,7
1,5 - 1,6
1,4 - 1,5
1,3 - 1,4
1,2 - 1,3
1,1 - 1,2
1,0 - 1,1
0,9 - 1
0,8 - 0,9
0,7 - 0,8
0,6 - 0,7
0,5 - 0,6
0,4 - 0,5
0,3 - 0,4
0,2 - 0,3
0,1 - 0,2
0 - 0,1

Ditches not only form part of the Beemster's cultural heritage, but also perform a number of additional functions, such as water storage, water drainage and parcel demarcation, as well as natural and landscape-related qualities. For purposes of increased efficiency, farmers sometimes find it advantageous to fill in ditches. The question whether a ditch can be allowed to disappear – or, indeed, whether one must be restored – is a complex one, in which cultural heritage is only one of the considerations. Our advice was to identify and inventory the relevant ditches and divide them into three classes, Class A, B or C. The ditches which appear in the copper engraving, those which still exist, as well as those which have been filled in, would be grouped in Class A. Those which are not included in the engraving, but are important for drainage, water storage or parcel demarcation, or because of their natural or landscape-related qualities, would fall under Class B. Those which do not score high for any of these criteria would be put in Class C. These ditches could be filled in, provided corresponding filled-in ditches in Class A with precisely the same respective lengths are re-dug elsewhere, in compensation. Given the present dynamics of compensation and tradable rights, this could result in every owner of a parcel containing a 'copper engraving ditch' re-digging such ditches and offering the rights pertaining to them for sale. As a result of this, the original ditches would suddenly have values which could not

DES BEEMSTERS water table, 2008.

DES BEEMSTERS cultural heritage is not a goal in itself, bringing the water system up to date must clearly not take place at the expense of the relevant qualities. Thus, cultural heritage formed a basis for studying current wishes and problems relating to the Beemster water system.

In a team effort in which, in addition to Bureau Des Beemsters, both the Water Board

and farmers participated, the wishes of farmers and other land users in the Beemster were identified and inventoried by means of meetings, open invitations and kitchen-table discussions. Water level adjustments, dam shifts, admission routes and drainage-route reductions were noted and studied. Under a deceptively clear system of straight waterways at right angles to one another, a hidden multicoloured map exhibiting differences in elevation and more than seventy different water levels and appurtenant hydraulic aids was discovered (see pp 146-147).

Once the Water Board had reduced its surface requirement to 10 hectares, it was no longer necessary for any farmland to be sacrificed. An engineering firm studied all of the wishes inventoried and assessed them in terms of feasibility, costs and any increases in proceeds which could result from more efficient land use as a result of modifications. The results of the study were presented to those who had registered their wishes. They, together with all others directly involved, were in turn asked to give their support to the measures in word and deed. Finally, in 2010, a package of measures was finalized with the Water Board, municipality and land owners, making possible a realization, in total, of almost twice the amount of additional water storage capacity needed.

Overview of measures to regulate the water system of the Beemster as a result of the **DES BEEMSTERS** project, 2008.
Source of map: Hoogheemraadschap Hollands Noorderkwartier/Maarten Poort

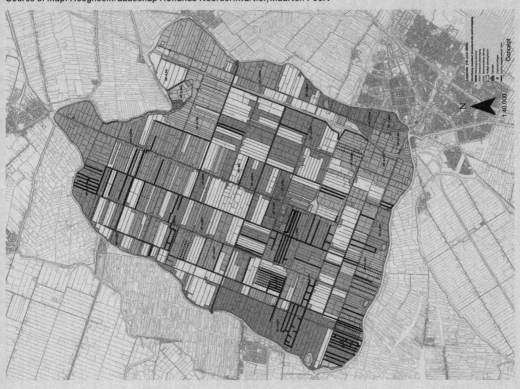

WATER MANAGEMENT

As its greatest task in the first year following its establishment, Bureau Des Beemsters took on the question of water management. As a result of climate change, the government is now also seeking more space for water storage in the Beemster. REDscape produced for *Des Beemsters I* four models for storing an additional 40 hectares of water in the Beemster, including one for a lake at the polder's lowest point or, alternatively, the former inundation fields of the UNESCO world heritage site, the Defence Line of Amsterdam. The models, however, met with a great deal of opposition. To the Beemsterites, sacrificing fertile farmland for water storage did not appear to be a discussable option. Based on this knowledge, as well as the results of its 'copper-engraving study', Bureau Des Beemsters designed a process in which cultural heritage could function as intermediary between the widely separated standpoints of the parties. **DES BEEMSTERS** convinced both land users and the Water Board of the importance of the relevant qualities, without focusing attention on its 'restoration'. Although for

but cause respect for them to increase. In the course of time, via these rules, the ditches of less importance would be exchanged for filled-in 'copper engraving ditches' without a loss of business efficiency or landscape-related quality.

DES BEEMSTERS

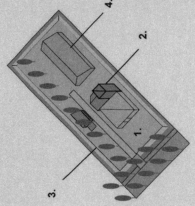

Essence of the new stead

1. Historical appearance (preserve)
2. Innovation and dynamism (new forms of living-working/experiment)
3. Landscape quality (improve and strengthen)
4. Agriculture (functional and added attention for architectural quality)

FARMSTEAD MAKERS

As is the case in a number of areas, the dynamics of the agricultural sector generate a great deal of change on the farmsteads in the Beemster. Landscape architect Patrick McCabe (REDscape) called attention to the specific qualities and development opportunities of the farmsteads as they relate to the development vision of **DES BEEMSTERS**. REDscape then investigated how such trends as scaling up, farmers

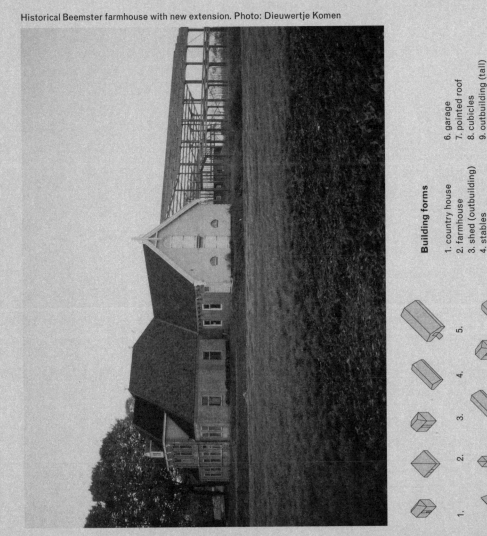

Historical Beemster farmhouse with new extension. Photo: Dieuwertje Komen

Building forms

1. country house
2. farmhouse
3. shed (outbuilding)
4. stables
5. agricultural shed
6. garage
7. pointed roof
8. cubicles
9. outbuilding (tall)
10. gardener's house

giving up farming, alternative economic activities and care and recreation can be applied successfully to the farmsteads. The vision of the Beemster farmstead which emerged from their study in no sense 'locks' the farmsteads 'shut', but rather, defines fundamental qualities, directions for development and a way for future adjustments to the farmsteads to influence these. In addition, this vision significantly simplifies future adjustments by shedding a much brighter light on the relevant limitations on development, and, as a result, on the opportunities for development on the farmsteads. Following its approval by the municipal council, the vision was laid down in the new zoning plan for the Beemster's outlying areas.

Acknowledgements

DES BEEMSTERS is a project by Bureau Venhuizen (Hans Venhuizen, Francien van Westrenen) commissioned by the municipality of Beemster, Milieufederatie and the Province of Noord-Holland (May 2005 – December 2010). In collaboration with Marinke Steenhuis and Paul Meurs (Steenhuis stedenbouw/ landschap), Patrick McCabe (REDscape Landscape and Urbanism) and Piet Snellaars (former head of the Department of Space in Beuningen, Gelderland).

With contributions from: Dieuwertje Komen (photography), Minke Themans in collaboration with Brenda Vonk Noordegraaf (design of reports), Harry Roenhorst and Han Hefting (municipality of Beemster).

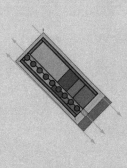

\+

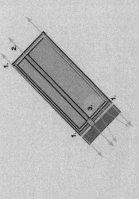

Functional layout

1. road zone = 14 m
2. garden = 20 m
3. living zone = 10 m
4. living-working zone = 15-35 m
5. working = 45 m (agricultural)

\+

Openness and sight lines

1. Keep ditches open (possible widening for water retention)
2. Keep view along road to land behind open
3. Keep view of front facade open

=

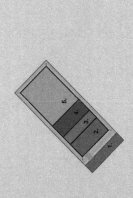

Design and landscape structure

1. The green foot: a 3-m green zone along the edge of the ditch that must remain free of buildings and roads
2. Greenery planted along the road

Basic rules of play

1. Handgrip: offers a clear grip for the integration of building volumes for various functions and the layout of the farmstead as a whole
2. Ambition level: creates a basic level of ambition for transformation of the plots

Illustrations: REDscape.

AMPHIBIOUS LIVING

GOUDA-TYPICAL

In the summer of 1998, Hans Venhuizen organized in Gouda the event **THE ART OF SETTLING.** Here, imaginary but realistic proposals at various levels of scale were presented concerning the future of the city. One of the questions that arose in the course of this project was: 'What architectural typology is typical of the city?' In arriving at what is typical for a region, people often directed attention towards the architectural objects that are unique to it, and that are associated with specific traditions. When we applied this approach to Gouda, we had to conclude that, whilst history has left behind a number of prominent elements in the city, its architectural typology nevertheless does not significantly differ from that of other Dutch cities – in other words, there is no such thing as *the Gouda-typical.* To try to understand the concept of the *region-typical,* one can begin by identifying the complex of criteria within which a typology comes about. For Gouda, this would be its windmills, sluices, polders, dikes and dike houses. All of these objects are testimony to a battle against the marshes – something which indeed typifies its entire region. From a technological standpoint, it goes against one's better judgement to want to build in Gouda. To prepare its boggy ground for building, it is necessary to drive in piles to a depth of at least 15 metres, after first having sprayed a substantial amount of sand on the ground. Pile driving results

Piles are driven into place to support the sewer that subsided during construction

competition were elaborated for a range of construction locations in the Province of Zuid-Holland. Generally speaking, designers are used to working in terms of a specific location, and to employing as starting points the unique manner in which the specific qualities of that location relate to one another. Whilst this often leads to designs especially suited to the locations for which they are intended, it by the same token makes difficult the distilling out of findings which could also function well at other locations. The **AMPHIBIOUS LIVING** competition, and the implementation phase which followed it, reversed this situation. First, the competition yielded a 'sample card' of possibilities for spatial planning approaches to boggy conditions. Then, the best suited solutions were applied to a number of locations in the Province of Zuid-Holland where boggy conditions play an important – if not the most important – role, and where the proposals can in turn be specially adapted to the particular characteristics of the locations in question.

The plan proposals were drawn up in cooperation with the designers of the selected entries. The proposals were then presented, at each respective location, to a forum of experts, who besides urban planners, administrators, water specialists and project developers, included residents of the relevant municipalities. Their reactions, questions and comments on amphibious living were in turn included in the resulting publication.

Styrofoam, and floating houses placed on the water, but, for the most part, such techniques are employed to realize *traditional* forms of living. **AMPHIBIOUS LIVING** combines all of these techniques, to enable the whole to be greater than the sum of its parts. This project, which in addition to the technical, ecological and designing aspects of working *with,* rather than *against* water, has brought the legal, political and, above all, mental prerequisites for am-

AMPHIBIOUS LIVING exhibition in the former pumping station Kinderdijk, Netherlands. Photo: Anne Bousema

in burying much capital under ground, and spraying with sand causes all characteristics of the landscape in question to be ruined, whilst this cannot even prevent subsidence in the long term. Thus, whilst generally being regarded as robust techniques, the closer one looks, the more spraying and pile driving appear to be approaches characterized by force, where in fact flexibility is needed. Put succinctly, Gouda-typical residential architecture is subject to the following conditions: 1) the capability to conform as required to Gouda's soggy soil conditions, 2) the obligation, when building, to preserve the existing landscape-related qualities to as great an extent as possible, 3) the need to build residential environments for the individual market, and 4) the capability to supply the demand for housing, as needed, whilst circumventing the national rules for dwelling distribution. These conditions inspired the development of a proposal for an 'amphibious dwelling.'

AMPHIBIOUS DYNAMICS

The amphibious dwelling provides a solution to the current enormous demand for housing-construction and shortage of usable land, and is a response to the growing importance attached to nature, landscape-related qualities, the environment, and a redefining our building culture. The techniques required for amphibious living already exist. At many locations, streets – and even gardens – are being laid on

phibious living to light, has become a plea for abandoning our compulsive need to manage water by means of fixed water levels and high dikes, and for the acceptance of weather influences, the tides and the seasons. Amphibious living is also a plea for the ultimate method of managing the continuously changing landscape: not by imposing our will on the landscape, but by taking optimum advantage of the qualities of a dynamic relationship between land and water: amphibious dynamics.

COMPETITION AND IMPLEMENTATION

What amphibious living can be, was clearly demonstrated by the entries to a competition organized by Bureau Venhuizen. In three categories, at all levels of scale – from entire 'delta plans' to allotment houses – more than 150 amphibious proposals were submitted. Whilst the competition's first two categories were open only to professionals, the third was open to anyone who was interested, regardless of their knowledge or expertise. (The first prize in the latter category was named after 'super-amateur' Willem Bos, who, long ago, in the discussion concerning the route of the high-speed train line, demonstrated an ability to exert a significant influence on spatial planning, doing so in an entirely uninhibited and unsuspicious manner.)
But the project did not end with the competition. In its second part, the most suitable ideas which had emerged from the

AMPHIBIOUS LIVING reveals the many possibilities for taking advantage of the conditions in boggy or tidal areas. It is a contribution to a process of reorienting the culture of subduing nature into one which takes advantage of existing qualities, and is thus a plea for a spatial planning based on continuity.

Image on previous page: Submission to the **AMPHIBIOUS LIVING** competition. Collage: Martijn Engelbregt and Herman van Bostelen

1800HRS·8TH·SEPTEMBER·2010

AMPHIBIOUS LIVING

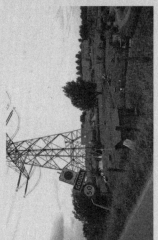

Gouda, Netherlands, from the dike.

In 1998, Hans Venhuizen organized in Gouda the event **THE ART OF SETTLING**, at which, at various levels of scale, imaginary but realistic proposals were made concerning the Gouda of the future. Based on numerous interviews with local historians, journalists, administrators and residents, the event consisted of four projects, distilled out and identified by Venhuizen:

INTRAPHERY: A rebirth for the outskirts of the city;

THE 6% SCHEME: Moroccan cultural traditions in a historic Dutch city;

THE SLOPPY WAY: Dwellings for the marshy polders of Gouda;

GOUDA MAKES SNAPSHOTS OF GOUDA: An out-of-the-ordinary photo competition.

For each of the first three projects, teams were brought together, each of which included at least one artist, one architect or urban planner and one theorist/publicist. The teams

'Le six-cientième Maroc'. Proposal for **THE 6% SCHEME** by Tom Frantzen

Sketch proposals for **THE SLOPPY WAY** amphibious neighbourhood by Marcel Musch and Nynke Jutten.

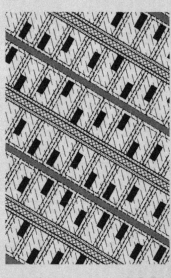

first carried out research in order to establish and inventory what already had been conceived and designed, and what the specific context of Gouda offers. In turn, the different themes were further developed in isolation, after which they were specifically applied to Gouda. The fourth portion of the event, the photo competition, literally involved residents of the city, who were asked to note qualities of their city and then treat their observations in publications and an exhibition.

THE 6% SCHEME and INTRAPHERY projects were not repeated subsequent to the event. However, the special method, developed in connection with the photo competition, for stimulating city dwellers to become involved in urban developments by means of observation, notation and competition, was used again in the concept-development method THE MAKING OF. THE SLOPPY WAY project ultimately resulted in the idea for AMPHIBIOUS LIVING, which included a competition, implementation project, website and publication.

Acknowledgements

AMPHIBIOUS LIVING emerged out of the project THE ART OF SETTLING by Hans Venhuizen in Gouda 1998 and under his supervision it was turned into a competition held in 2000 by Kunstgebouw in collaboration with Stichting Amfibisch Wonen.

Concept management: Bureau Venhuizen, Hans Venhuizen, Maureen Timmermans, Irmin Eggens, Caroline Wolf, Margot Lieftinck.

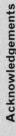

GOUDA MAKES SNAPESHOTS OF GOUDA, a prize-winning series of photos by Anneke de Jong from Gouda.

Image on previous page: Examples of the projects for AMPHIBIOUS LIVING in Barendrecht, Netherlands, by Lucas Verweij, Dennis Moet, Tom Mossel, Martijn Schoots, Van Velzen La Feber Bonneur Architecten, Liza Mackenzie and Neil Davidson, 2000.
Image on next page: You shouldn't actually want to build in Gouda at all. The sign reads: Cyclists dismount.

FIETSERS
AFSTAPPEN

THE MAKING OF

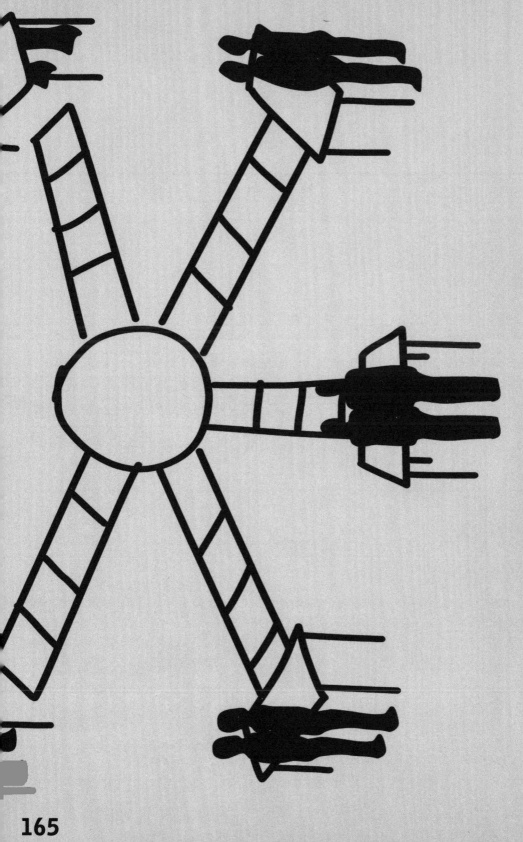

THE MAKING OF

CREATIVE THOUGHT PROCESS

The game THE MAKING OF is a method for initiating a creative thought process amongst parties affected by or interested in a process of (spatial) change. The method can be deployed to especially good effect in the second phase of such a process. Once the relevant qualities, wishes and ideas have been compiled using questionnaires, interviews and studies, the game facilitates both their examination and coherent consideration, from which, in turn, the prerequisites for the change in question can emerge. The method involves the (many) interested parties involved in the process of change by simultaneously informing the participants concerning future changes, consulting with them about those changes and letting them form part of the changes. THE MAKING OF is also a good way to involve residents in processes of change in their living environment.

COMPLEXITY OF SPATIAL PLANNING

Processes of (spatial) change are by definition complicated tasks, as they necessitate bringing the interests of many people, governments, companies and representatives together with the possibilities of a given context, the history of that context, as well as the rules and regulations in force there. New plans not only have to be technically feasible,

THE MAKING OF for 'Maak Plaats', Netherlands Architecture Institute, Rotterdam, April 2009. Photos: Michaela Stegerwald and Joost Maaskant

and to have a sufficient support base, but must also be financially feasible. All of the tasks surrounding the spatial planning of this country are interconnected, and the question whether something is beautiful typically plays either a very small role, or even none at all. The complexity of spatial planning ensures that only a very limited number of persons have a clear picture of it, making it more and more important for these persons to know the opinions and wishes of as many people as possible, in order to be able to create better plans. But due to the complexities involved, discussions on spatial changes are frequently dominated by self-interest or the question as to whether something is beautiful or ugly. To gather information from people who are generally not involved in a professional capacity with the spatial planning of this country, it is necessary for these people to acquire the requisite knowledge for forming opinions and arriving at good proposals. This is what THE MAKING OF facilitates. It makes complicated situations transparent and ensures that everyone involved can contribute his/her ideas. THE MAKING OF prevents discussions from stranding in the 'beautiful or ugly' zone, and focuses attention on the task preceding spatial design. It stimulates participants to conceive of innovative proposals concerning issues in the area of spatial planning, and confronts them with the complexity of a design task, not by explaining it but by making them a part of it.

GAME MATRIX

As part of the game, a voluminous package of opinions, wishes, initiatives, threats and requisite interventions concerning the process of change involved is compiled and synopsized. In turn, this information is divided into two packages. The one group consists of the 'ambitions' which in the future will result in the relevant changes. They include necessary interventions, such as more houses or more roads, as well as working towards a desirable change in mentality in respect of, for example, automobile use. These ambitions set the relevant spatial changes in motion. The other group consists of the so-called phenomena. In and of themselves, these do not set a process of change in motion, but give colour, direction and guidance to such a process. Important phenomena are, for example, the country's cultural heritage or the support base required for change. Because spatial changes are subject to numerous influences, a vast number of things can be phenomena. From pride about the automobile to our expensive petrol, and from prosperity to fine particles: all of these facets exert a strong influence on the decisions which must eventually be taken concerning the spatial planning of this country.
Once they are brought together in a matrix, the ambitions and phenomena form the point of departure for the game THE MAKING OF. The matrix provides an

overall picture of the existing situation, which is about to change. As already mentioned, there is virtually no one who can encompass the entire picture. For this reason, we commence the game THE MAKING OF, by placing a few combinations of ambitions and phenomena in the matrix.

Image on pp 164-165: illustration by Designbureau 75B, Rotterdam
Image on previous page: THE MAKING OF game arena. Photo: Dieuwertje Komen

THE MAKING OF

Introduction in the game setting

Preliminary investigation

Making proposals

Formulating objections

After the lobby there is one winning proposal

Debating the objections

Lobby

Presenting proposals

Objections on the game floor

The jury votes

Photos: Michaela Stegerwald and Joost Maaskant

HOW THE GAME IS ORGANIZED

Reception

A round of THE MAKING OF is, by definition, played in one's own, special setting. The decor for the game is mobile and can be set up in a space near the situation under consideration. THE MAKING OF calls for a minimum of eight and a maximum of sixty participants. At their reception in the game environment, the participants are divided into five teams. An effort should be made to avoid assigning friends, colleagues and contemporaries to the same team.

The game floor

The playing field set up in the space is a large circle, 6 metres in diameter. Five tables, in the colours blue, red, yellow, purple and green are arranged at the circle's circumference. A strip 250 cm long and 40 cm wide, with sections in the latter five colours, runs from the tables to the midpoint of the circle. The moderator has complete freedom of movement over the entire playing field. The participants sit behind the five tables.

Introduction

By way of an introduction, an overview of the rules is presented using PowerPoint. The rules are explained in some detail. Further, the ambitions and phenomena which have been formulated are given a brief introduction. In this way, the participants become familiar with the different facets of the situation.

teams, but there is no debating at this point in the game.

Game sheet to note the proposals by other teams (above) and to note objections against the other teams (below).

The Making Of ®

A proposal by team: ☐ red ☐ blue ☐ yellow ☐ purple ☐ green

Ambition

Phenomenon

Proposal by the team

Objections to the proposal

The Making Of ®

Notice of objection

Objections against red team   ☐ 1   ☐ 2

Objections against blue team   ☐ 1   ☐ 2

Jury

The moderator ensures that the debate is carried on in a proper manner, and lets each team formulate its objections and answers, respectively. If the teams fail to reach agreement, the jury decides. The jury can be changed from situation to situation. It can consist of one member: a judge. Having heard all of the different arguments, the judge can render a wise decision as to whether the relevant objections are justified or not. The jury can also be comprised of a number of experts in the area in question, or of all of the 'experience experts' present, in other words, the public. In the case of a jury made up of the public, it will be determined by a majority of the votes cast whether the objections will be maintained or rejected. The moderator can first ask the opinions of the experts present, or poll the opinion of the public, after which the jury votes by a show of hands.

Lobbies

Good proposals win on the basis of good argumentation, attractive presentations or because they offer an appealing perspective. In reality, one's lobby plays a central role in such decisions: who your friends are and what their position is are the deciding factors when it comes to which proposal wins. If the objections of one or more teams have been rejected and their pawn has reached the middle, lobby tickets are distributed to all jury members. Through how they distribute these, the

Devising proposals

From the matrix, each group receives two combinations of an ambition and phenomenon as an assignment. The groups withdraw into different corners of the room to devise proposals in order to compete to see which group can come up with the most successful ambition/phenomenon combination. They devise proposals based on the questions on the proposal form. The teams must opt for a proposal and work it out as best they can within the time allotted to them. Materials for writing, drawing, building and taking photos are provided to all the teams.

Proposal form

A proposal form has been developed for the purpose of introducing the task, and calling the attention of the participants to its different facets. On it, they can describe their proposal and add a drawing and catchy slogan (see pp 176-177).

Presenting the proposal

After having produced their proposals, the teams again come together in the arena, take their seats behind their respective tables and present their proposals to one another. In addition to having a convincing proposal, the strength of one's argumentation and the attractiveness of one's presentation are of great importance. The moderator and any experts who may be present may ask questions of the

First circle your own team

You can lodge a maximum of three objections as follows:
1 x 1 objection against a proposal by a team
1 x 2 objections against a proposal by a team
This means that two proposals escape without objections.

Submitting objections

Rather than entering directly into a debate on a given proposal, the other teams indicate on a special form as many objections as possible to the proposal under discussion. After the presentations have all been given, the teams indicate how many objections they have listed concerning the other proposals. The number of objections the teams may direct to each other is limited, and can change from situation to situation.

Debate

The objections are displayed on the game floor, between the different teams, by placing 'objection pawns' on the coloured areas corresponding to the respective teams registering objections. Now it is literally possible to see which proposals have received many objections from the other teams, and which few. The order of the coloured areas in the 'circuit' which each team has before it determines the order in which the teams will debate with one another. A given objecting team formulates its objections; in turn, the team to which these objections have been addressed has an opportunity to defend itself.

members express their preference for one or more proposals. Provided they have sufficient lobbyists, the teams can neutralize objections without the need to present argumentation.

Winner

Ultimately, one team will succeed in becoming the first to shed all of the objections against it, and to keep the most lobby influence. This team is the winner of **THE MAKING OF**, and receives a prize chosen especially for this occasion, which can range from an award cup or trophy to a book or simply a hearty handshake.

Results

It is not always the best proposal that emerges as winner; the proposal to which the other teams have the fewest objections is not always the one which best captures the imagination. In addition, argumentation and debating skills, successful manipulation of the jury *and* luck in accumulating lobby support are, as discussed above, very important factors.

After one or more rounds have been played, Bureau Venhuizen is able to process all of the proposals and objections into a coherent design brief, which can now serve as a motor for the process of change. This plan for change (i.e., the design brief) can in turn be recognized and supported by numerous interested parties.

THE MAKING OF

TEAM ROOD – Den Haag

VOORSTEL: slimme kassen meer ruimte

CLEVER GREENHOUSES Crops no longer grow on the ground. Raise the greenhouses and store water below or cultivate 'dark crops' there.

TEAM GROEN – Utrecht

VOORSTEL: vinexie is sexy

SIMPLY HAPPY IN THE VINEX NEIGHBOURHOOD For it's a nice place to be.

TEAM ORANJE

VOORSTEL: scaten chillen

TEAM PAARS

VOORSTEL: slimme vuilnisbelt werkgelegenheid

THE SQUARE CREATES EMPLOYMENT Neighbourhood residents keep an eye on the square with barbecue, light masts and sanitary facilities.

TEAM ORANJE – Den Haag

VOORSTEL: duifje mijn duifje

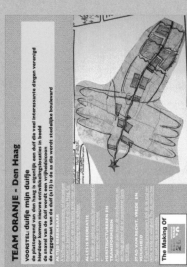

MY SWEET DOVE The Hague, city of peace and justice, can develop its plan so that a peace dove emerges.

TEAM PAARS – Amsterdam

VOORSTEL: creeer ruimte door te bouwen

TEAM BLAUW

VOORSTEL: Johan (de bult) werkgelegenheid

EDIBLE CITY Use all the space you have in the city to cultivate crops.

TEAM BLAUW

VOORSTEL: Sixtusplein waar sporten fijn kan zijn. Het FITNESSPLEIN meer daden dan woorden

FITNESS SQUARE Action, not words. Lots of sport on the square and a roof for when it rains.

TEAM ROOD – Almere

VOORSTEL: ZZP ict want zzp wordt zmp

FREELANCERS BECOME EMPLOYERS Foster the one-man businesses in the city, for they will soon create employment for others.

TEAM BLAUW

VOORSTEL: Spelen en rusten
ook het schoolplein or bij zo bereiken
en andere plaatsen zijn semi-professional met demontabile speeltoestellen
sanitaire voorzieningen, surveillance
het plein wordt beter beruikbaar as ingedeeld in eilanden met wereldpoorten gethematiseerd
achtergrond
om zonnestrand met wat voor carrosje
overzicht vanaf de duinrimp

Ambitie – Knotsgek

WORLD GATEWAYS Set up various gates on the square that stand for the different cultures in the neighbourhood.

TEAM ORANJE

VOORSTEL: het WE (wij) court – alles is mogelijk
het troctcloir wordt een mooie laan
links een sloteir mob een speel fontaintje
middenin een kraijbek court
rechts vrij spelen voorral ook voor meisjes
dusintsjprop voor materraq op het middenveld
De regels op een borch johan idarqgek
een gezlikre buurtbrwoner past op

THE WE COURT Design a luxury square supervised by the residents themselves.

SKATING AND CHILLING Build a stand containing all sorts of amenities.

MAKE SPACE BY BUILDING Make the city compact and keep as much green as possible in the area.

TEAM GROEN – Almere

VOORSTEL: ALMERE BEN JE SAMEN
UGLY BETTY is lelijk, maar wel lief relaties zijn belangrijker dan schoonheid
Almere richt zich op zorg en voeding:
technologie, productie, biologische landbouw uit het achterland én de voortuin
almere wordt een superdorp met toprestaurants rondom topscholen
je bent wat je bent en dat is super
superstrand, superscholen en superwijken

SEABOTTON VALLEY
A Dutch version...

DE LELIJSTE STAD VAN NETERLAND
F Gek...

ALMERE ALTOGETHER The city is ugly and unpopular perhaps, but it is sweet, and that's more important than beauty.

TEAM ROOD – Rotterdam

VOORSTEL: alles van hoeksche waarde is weergaloos
wat is voor een stedeling het landschap waard
recreeëren, open landschap!
water: drijvende woningen in woeste rivieren
blauwe stad is goed!
Hoeksche waard blijft hetzelfde
het zuiden wordt een écht cultuurlandschap
boeren eruit als ze willen grienden en vrij water – betaald door stijging onroerend goed
aardappelen en uien komen ergens anders vandaan
energieopwekking/zoet en zout
educatie voor mensen uit de...

WAT IS HET HOEKSCHE WAARD
A plek die...

HET WATER KOMT VAN BOVEN
F Gek wat...

HOEKSCHE WAARD IS UNRIVALLED Rotterdam, look after your landscape to the south and let it develop cautiously.

FEASIBLE CREATIVE Let's first clean up the square and then see what we're going to do.

TEAM BLAUW

VOORSTEL: de haalbaarheid van de creativiteit
we beginnen met een schoonmaakactie
en hebben geen events bedacht, het moet een initiatief zijn van buurtbewoners
buurtinitiatief met subsidie als ideeënmachine
een platform bij het...
speeltoestollen uitvrolosten met andere plainen
een kunstgrasvlakte zonder lijnen

TEAM GROEN

VOORSTEL:
water op het plein water is lovendig en stroomt dat zorgt voor beweging
wat is voor een stedeling een sloteir mob een fontaine ook licht geeft in de nacht, beton rond de fontein in de winter is er geen water maar
kun je er skaten.
meer groen bij en gras

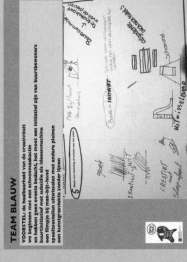

WATER Add water to the square; that makes it lively and dynamic.

Game form to elaborate the combination between ambition and phenomenon into a proposal.
Design version by Bureau Venhuizen based on an original design by Design Bureau 75B, Rotterdam

THE MAKING OF

Date: Team:

1 AMBITION

PHENOMENON

2 What does the ambition make you think of?

10 Make a drawing of your proposal.

9 Elaborate your proposal and describe it in ten sentences.

8 Think of a catchy slogan for your proposal.

The Making Of® ®

Credits
The Making Of is a concept development game for 5 to 50 participants
from 8 to 8 to 88 years old and was developed by Hans Venhuizen
© 2001/2009 Bureau Venhuizen – wwwbureauvenhuizen.com

u recognize the phenomenon?

4 Write down a few ideas that connect the ambition to the phenomenon.

5 Do you know of comparable situations that have worked well?

What objections do you expect from others?

6 Indicate how feasible your proposal is and how long it will take to realize it.

THE MAKING OF

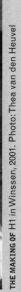

THE MAKING OF H1 in Winssen, 2001. Photo: Thea van den Heuvel

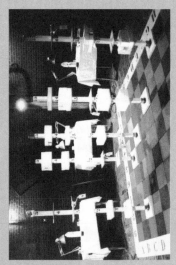

First game décor **THE MAKING OF** in Beuningen, 2000.
Photo: Inge Hoonte

THE MAKING OF at 'Maak ons Land', Netherlands Architecture Institute, Rotterdam, October 2008. Photo: Maarten Laupman

THE MAKING OF in the Beemster, September 2005. Photo: Dieuwertje Komen

THE MAKING OF for 'Maak Plaats', Netherlands Architecture Institute, Rotterdam, April 2009. Photo: Michaela Stegerwald and Joost Maaskant

THE MAKING OF

BACKGROUND

THE MAKING OF was developed in 2000 as part of THE INVENTION OF THE FLOOD PLAIN MODEL, a project commissioned by the Municipality of Beuningen (Gelderland). In early 2000, the From-Weurt-to-Deest Foundation invited Bureau Venhuizen to organize a project with the aim of creating a connection between art and the flood plain landscape. For this purpose, Hans Venhuizen distilled from the flood plain landscape its essential aspects, and integrated them in the Flood Plain Model.

The Flood Plain Model is based on a flexible alliance with the elements. As such, it is a worthy successor to the obsolete, consultation model from the world of politics known as the Polder Model, or 'the third way'. Both of these models developed in connection with human interaction with water, but whereas the Polder Model is based on a struggle against water and the complete subduing of nature, the Flood Plain Model treats nature as a fertile ground with which to build. This model is not based on the form which the landscape has been *given*, but rather, how this form has *developed*.

The man-made landscape behind the dike, the area from Weurt to Deest, has been flooded by such large-scale spatial developments as residential construction projects, infrastructural projects and sand excavations. The Flood Plain Model set in motion a sedimentation process resulting in the distilling out of

For the rounds of the game played around Mheen Park in Apeldoorn, a new decor, representing a further development of the rubber version, but featuring practical improvements for both moderator and participants, was produced by Chris Koens. The decor for this version, which, after Apeldoorn, was deployed in such locations as Berlin Marzahn, the Beemster, the Wieringermeer, Breda-Noordoost and Rotterdam-Hoogvliet, was, in addition, both easy to use and to transport.

In 2009, THE MAKING OF formed part of the event and exhibition 'Maak ons Land' ('Make our Country'), at the Netherlands Architecture Institute. Here, in the course of six months, some forty rounds involving current spatial planning themes were played, in a decor designed by the artists' group, Observatorium.

THE MAKING OF in Berlin Marzahn, Germany, 2002. Illustration: Beeldleveranciers

Acknowledgements

The first version of THE MAKING OF was created in 2000–2002 as part of the project THE INVENTION OF THE FLOOD PLAIN MODEL, commissioned by the From Weurt to Deest Foundation, Beuningen. Concept management: Hans Venhuizen.

From 2001 to 2010 about 800 people played THE MAKING OF in over 65 rounds, and at least 80 people contributed through workshops,

180

design, visualization, advice, moderators, the role of jury and judge, financing, organization and practical support. THE MAKING OF is particularly indebted to a number of these people: Hilde de Bruijn, Marieke Berkers, Inge Hoonte, Caroline Wolf, Max Daniel, Francien van Westrenen, Lucas Verweij, Peti Buchel, Carolien Feldbrugge, Thea van den Heuvel, Margit Schuster, KRILL, Bernard Colenbrander, Hans van Houwelingen, Tjerk Ruimschotel, Guus van der Heiden, Piet Snellaars, Belvedere (Ministries of VROM, OCW and LNV), Municipality of Beuningen, Stichting van Weurt tot Deest, Province of Gelderland, Prins Bernhard Cultuurfonds, VSBfonds, Bouwfonds, Cultuurfonds Bank Nederlandse Gemeenten, UrbanPlan Berlin, Saskia Visser, Emma Gossink, Martin Leclercq, Chris Koens, Dieuwertje Komen, Werkgroep Maak Mheenpark Mooi en Actiegroep Behoud Mheenpark, Maarten van Wesemael, Harry Roenhorst, Municipality of Beemster, Province of Zuid-Holland, Netherlands Architecture Institute, Anneke Abhelakh, Ole Bouman, Ferry Piekart, Bas Rellum, Mieke Dings, Martine Zoeteman, Linda Vlassenrood, Observatorium, Bert van Meggelen, David ter Avest, Leo van Loon, Michaela Stegerwald, John van de Wetering, Erfgoedhuis ZH, AORTA, STROOM Den Haag, AIR Rotterdam, Municipality of Breda, Henk Ovink, Tom Maas, Saskia Newrly, Bart Vink, YMERE, MAB, KNCH, Ellen Klaus, Municipality of Wieringermeer.

THE MAKING OF for 'Maak Plaats', Netherlands Architecture Institute, Rotterdam, April 2009. Illustration: Michaela Stegerwald

THE MAKING OF H1 in Winssen, 2001. Illustration: Buro Zijaanzicht

(current) cultural-heritage qualities suited to play a leading role regarding current interventions in the area. These qualities are developed and communicated in such a manner that they are able to contribute to the cultural continuity of this constantly changing landscape. To investigate what qualities have been able to generate this continuity, Hans Venhuizen developed the game THE MAKING OF. Under the title, THE MAKING OF: FROM WEURT TO DEEST, we, together with residents and interested parties, first played the game in the historic windmill of Beuningen, Gelderland. The first version of the game's decor consisted of a literal 'translation' of the matrix on the floor of the windmill. The participants placed their proposals, and their respective opponents their objections, on this matrix. The game was played using a matrix composed of the results from the Flood Plain Project.

THE MAKING OF

Following its premiere in Beuningen, THE MAKING OF was used as a method for involving residents in the planning of a large-scale sand excavation near the village of Winssen. The game underwent further development, and was given a second decor, made from rubber mats and featuring circuits consisting of colour areas, produced by the KRILL firm of architects. On these colour areas, opponents placed their objections against the proposals made by the teams.

Image on next page: THE MAKING OF at 'Maak ons Land', Netherlands Architecture Institute, Rotterdam, October 2008. Photo: Maarten Laupman

DOING-AS-IF

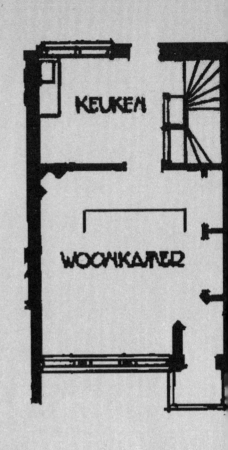

KEUKEN

WOONKAMER

BEGA

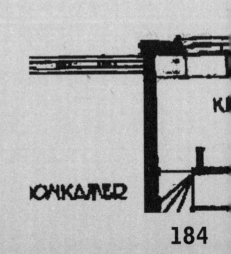

KE

OONKAMER

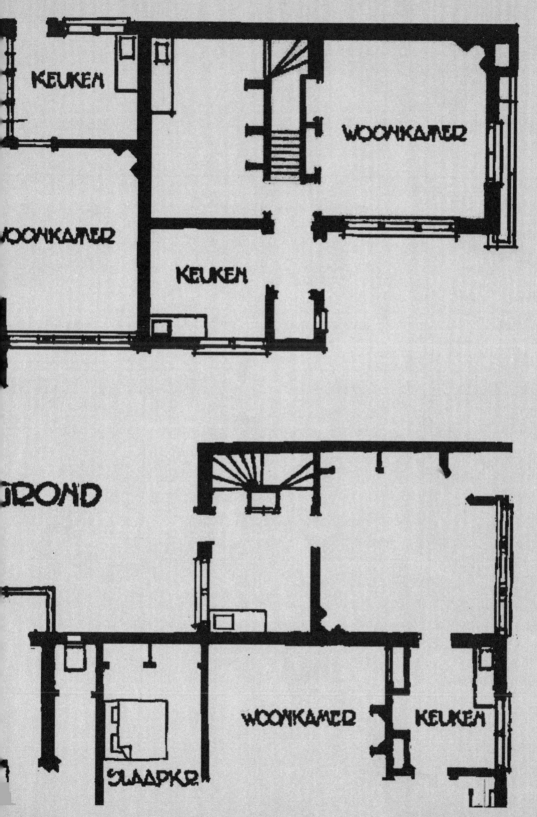

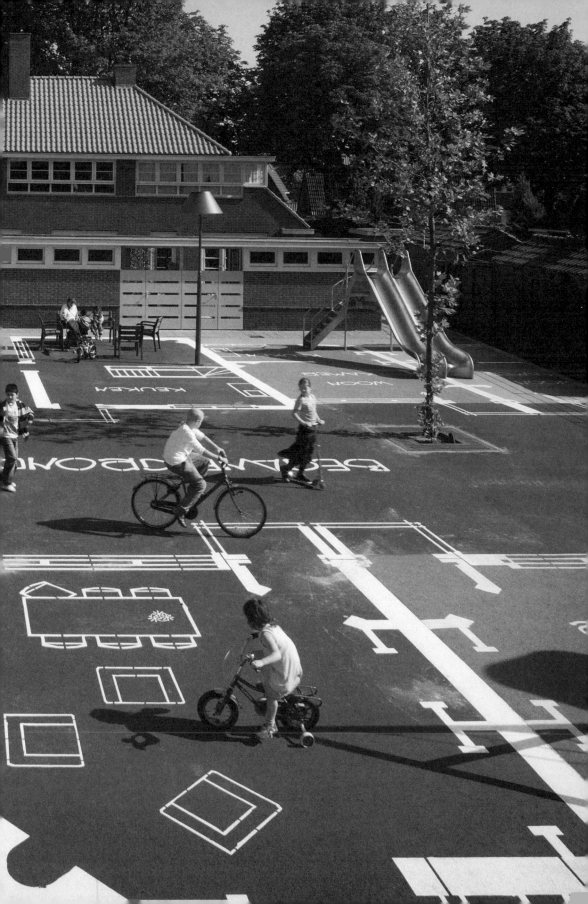

DOING-AS-IF

Since much residential architecture originally designed in the 1930s by city architect Willem Marinus Dudok had disappeared from the Liebergen section of Hilversum, under the initiative 'Dudok revisited', demolished Dudok dwellings were re-erected under the supervision of architect Hans Ruijssenaars. Going a step further, Ruijssenaars ensured that the district would become even more Dudokian than it ever had been. The result was spectacular: a kind of 'Dudok 2.0' in which it was impossible to detect what was old and what was new. In draughting his master-plan, Ruijssenaars studied historical photos of the

Van 't Hoffplein in Hilversum, 1930.
Photo: Streekarchief Gooi en Vechtstreek

When the floor plans, taken from Dudok's original drawings at a scale of 1:1, are plotted on the inner court, the first thing one notices is how small these original dwellings were. The living room, kitchen and bedroom are all immediately recognisable from the drawing. Naturally, the playground equipment takes complete advantage of the floor plans: the bench and lamps are in the living room, the refuse bin in the kitchen, the shack in the garden; the swing hangs between the sliding doors and the slide starts in the staircase. The legally required soft floors around the equipment were easy to integrate. The original floor plans clearly offer play opportunities and directly evoke something of the architecture of Dudok in its original surroundings, but without cultural-heritage references. Thus, the playground constitutes a kind of 'Dudok for beginners'. It re-uses a typical Dudok quality in an entirely foreign context.

second proposal, one for a playground, in the inner court, did manage to get through.

AS-IF INTERIORS, AS-IF DWELLINGS

Ruijssenaars recognized and respected the existing qualities of Dudok's dwellings, but, to meet present-day needs nevertheless introduced modifications, the most prominent of which being those to their floor plans. As a way of showing how these dwellings looked in Dudok's day, Hans Venhuizen proposed incorporating floor plans by Dudok in the design of the above mentioned playground.

Illustration: Olivier Scheffer

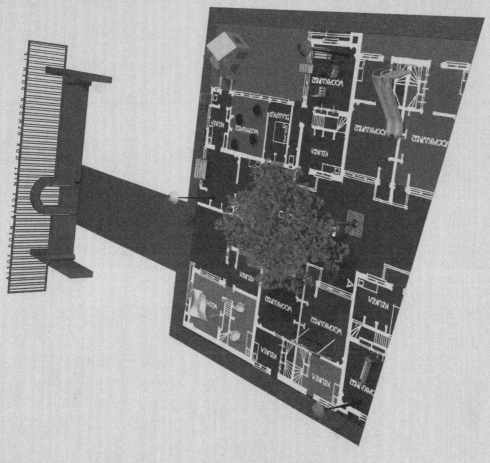

district in great detail and saw that the public space was unusually empty. Even though in the early 1930s, when these photos had been made, virtually no one had an automobile, there were hardly any public amenities, and the site's greenery had only just been planted, this did not stop Ruijssenaars from wanting to restore the 'original' situation down to the last detail. Shrubs were removed, limits were placed on parking, and the playground that had existed in the middle of the green area of Van 't Hoff Square was also removed. This was the situation when Hans Venhuizen was commissioned to devise proposals for how art and culture could be deployed in this environment. As Ruijssenaars' plans were already being implemented at the time, and it was too late for a significant intervention in the planning for the area, my first proposal was cosmetic in nature. To guarantee the desired appearance for the square in both summer and winter, and even under the worst possible drought conditions, Hans Venhuizen proposed to make the grass cover of Van 't Hoff Square of synthetic grass: always green and low-maintenance. By way of an ironic reference to the black & white photos which served as the basis for the plans for the square, a somewhat greyish synthetic grass cover could even be opted for. To my great surprise, though, the Municipality of Hilversum informed me that, in its experience, a synthetic grass cover requires more maintenance than real grass, and thus, this proposal was not realized. My

Previous page: Photo Jannes Linders

DOING-AS-IF

Illustration: Olivier Scheffer

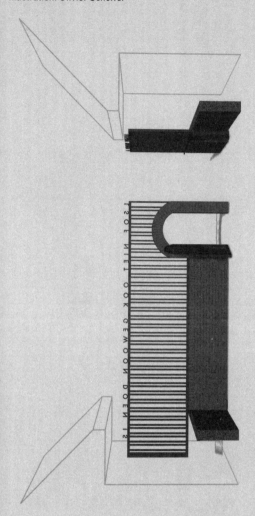

The playground is only accessible in the daytime to parents with children through the age of eight. The terrain is closed off on all sides and only accessible through a gate, whose design is based on one of the most beautiful gates ever designed by Dudok, that of the Noorderbegraafplaats cemetery in Hilversum. The gate bears the text: 'AS THOUGH DOING-AS-IF WERE NOT ALSO SIMPLY DOING' ('ALSOF DOEN ALSOF NIET OOK GEWOON DOEN IS'), which one sees upon leaving the playground. After the children have enjoyed themselves in the as-if interiors of the as-if dwellings, this text has an extraordinarily comforting effect on the young reader, for in 'doing as if', children are training their ability to function in the grown-up world. For grown-ups, it should have more the character of a warning, as they are not leaving the 'do as if'-world, but are re-entering the very surroundings in which 'doing as if' (e.g., building in a historicizing manner) has now become extraordinarily ordinary.

Acknowledgements
The playground was developed in 2005/2006 by Bureau Venhuizen in cooperation with Joost Volkers, for the Municipality of Hilversum, Office of Urban Development.

Design: Hans Venhuizen with the assistance of Olivier Scheffer, Joost Volkers and Wigger Bierma. The project was designed and executed for the Municipality of Hilversum and was in part made possible through (financial) support from the Province of Noord-Holland.

DOING-AS-IF

Photo: Jannes Linders

194

Photo: Jannes Linders

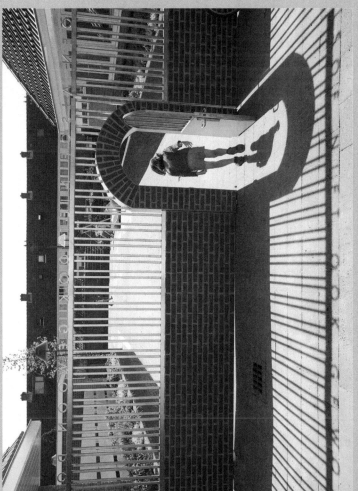

Photo: Jannes Linders

BULB

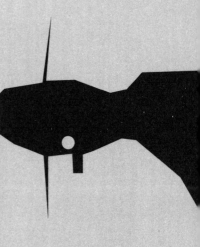

BULB

In **SOUL AND SOIL: CULTURAL SPATIAL PLANNING IN THE DUNE AND BULB REGION,** Bureau Venhuizen studied the role that historic and current cultural heritage will play in the future spatial planning of the Dune and Bulb Region. This was done in the context of a two-year programme, comprising three successive phases: survey, competition and implementation. All interested parties with respect to spatial planning – urban designers, spatial planners, (cultural) historians, (landscape) architects, artists, administrators and residents – were represented in each of these phases.

The programme's point of departure was the conviction that objects and structures have the best chance of continuing to exist if they are re-used. This is why the study included a search for continuity in the value and usefulness of remnants of the past. In the first phase of the study, these remnants were inventoried as cultural heritage characteristics and qualities, landscape developments and current bottle-necks. Some remnants were subjected to further investigation in research assignments, others served as the basis for one of the three competitions. In turn, in cooperation with the competition winners and municipalities, research was carried out into the possibilities for actually realizing the proposals.

All relevant research, essays, photographic assignments, reflections, competition results and their elaborations were reproduced in the catalogue published in connection with the project. In addition, the collected material

where they live and the work they do; how they build their businesses and how they plan their villages; how they travel through the area and what they leave behind; that there are many buildings and people at the one location and none at the other. By searching in the landscape, via the aerial photo of the area, you can gather information about it. Below the aerial photo, you will also find historical maps of the area. In this way, you can compare the landscape as it is today with how it once was, and you can see how the landscape came to be as it is today.

The landscape not only has a past and a present but also a future. The Dune and Bulb Region has many desires for new residential and commercial architecture and roads, as well as nature and recreation areas. These desires can also be called ambitions. Such ambitions are not always easy to recognize when looking at the landscape, as they have yet to be realized. **BULB** presents the seven most relevant of these ambitions all in a row. They are all named at the top of the map and include heritage, tourism and landscape. In realizing these ambitions, the identity of the area involved can play an important role. Such an identity is composed of a range of different characteristics from the past and present. For **BULB,** six of these characteristics are given the status of so-called phenomena. They are located on the right, beside the map, and include F1 – the Bulb Sheds, F2 – the Archaeology, or F3 – the Disorderly Landscape.

Game board

Today

1949

1900

1850

1600

0

was adapted for use in a special educational website, www.bulb-web.nl.

WWW.BULB.NL

On www.bulb-web.nl., school children can discover the past, present and future of their region. On the site, they encounter a treasure-trove of information, in the form of maps, informative items, animations, games, photos, film fragments and assignments. **BULB** is an interdisciplinary website suitable for use for the subjects geography, history, social studies and cultural studies. The website's education-al content is based on the material and *imma-terial* findings, facts, ideas and designs that resulted from the project **SOUL AND SOIL**. The material was adapted and rewritten for **BULB** and consists, amongst other things, of short texts, photos, film excerpts, drawings and animations. The website's objective is to make pupils aware of the history of their own region and show them how that history can be used in the future. Log onto: www.bulb-web.nl. and log in as ADMIN, using the password BLUB.

READ THE LANDSCAPE

One can learn much about the Dune and Bulb Region and its history by reading books or going online. But the stories and histories in which the region is rich can also be read directly from the landscape. For example: how the landscape is used, how people live there,

SEARCH ON THE MAP

The aerial photo of the Dune and Bulb Region occupies a central position on the board. Below it, you can see the points with the years from the historical maps hidden under the aerial photo. Above the photo are the seven most important ambitions of the region. If you click on one of these ambitions, you will be able to read a short description of it. If you activate an ambition, a number of white and yellow dots will appear on the map if you zoom in closely on the aerial photo.

The white dots contain general information on the region. Via the questions connected to the white dots, you can earn points which you will need later. If a question is about history, if you click on it, the appropriate historical map will appear. You can also look for dots on the historical maps. You can see how many points you have won under the aerial photo. The yellow dots contain specific information concerning the ambition in question and the so-called phenomenon which could play a role in its regard. In this phenomenon, a range of characteristics from the past and present have been collected which typify the identity of the area in question. The six phenomena can be found to the right of the aerial photo. If you click on them, relevant information will appear. The yellow dots are very important for collecting the requisite knowledge points on the scoreboard. The link to the scoreboard can also be found under the aerial photo.

199

BULB

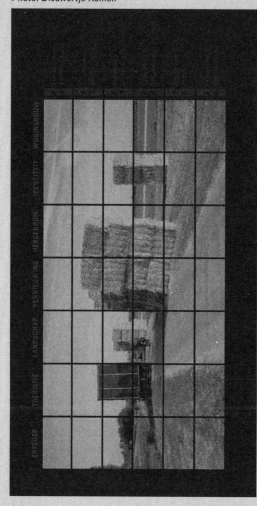

Still from BULB-WEB.nl website. Design: Antenna-Men.
Photo: Dieuwertje Komen

AMBITIONS

Heritage

The Dune and Bulb Region has not always been like it is now. The landscape and the built surroundings develop constantly under the influence of the economy, politics and the environment. Developments occur at such a fast pace today that it's easy to forget how things used to be, for example in the time your grandparents were young. And precisely because the surroundings change so quickly, there is more and more attention for the history and the remains of the past. For our cultural history tells us not only about the past but also about today.

– Show respect for history in the rapidly changing landscape.

Tourism

Up to 3 or 4 million tourists come to the Dune and Bulb Region every year. More than half the region's economy is dependent on tourism. Tourists don't just come for the Keukenhof flower garden but also for the beach and the unique landscape. The number of visitors is dropping at present and the popularity of traditional bulb tourism is declining.

– Let the tourism in the region grow further.

Landscape

In the Teylingen Pact the ten municipalities in the Bulb Region are going to work together to prevent the region's landscape from getting any uglier. For in recent years it's all got a bit untidy with all those bigger company buildings, greenhouses and new businesses. You can't look far across the landscape any more without some structure blocking your view. All sorts of attempts are being made to make the Bulb Region more beautiful.

– Make the landscape of the region more beautiful.

Innovation

The Bulb Region is famous for the drive to innovate and experiment. Constant innovation made the area rich in the past, and it is necessary once more for the economy of the area. What you see are the bulbs in the field, but what

SCOREBOARD

The scoreboard is comprised of all relevant ambitions (above) and all relevant phenomena (right). If you activate an ambition, you will get six squares containing possible combinations with phenomena. Once you have found enough yellow dots *and* you have collected enough points, you can open a square. Below in the picture, you can see how many yellow dots or points you still need to collect in order to be able to open that square on the scoreboard. Here, it is not only a question of how many yellow dots you already have; for some squares, you must find very specific dots, which occur only once on the map.

Behind the squares on the scoreboard, you can find the projects in which an ambition has been formed by the phenomenon with which it is associated. These are all extremely special and promising projects for the Dune and Bulb Region, e.g., competitions concerning new bulb sheds or projects about how landscape can be created using refuse, ones about how the development of the Keukenhof flower garden and ones about shipwrecks. Eighteen squares have projects with games behind them. Behind the other twenty-four are opportunities for special future projects. But perhaps you will have to design these yourself.

it's really about are the often invisible innovations. Those innovations occur in the area of climate control, storage, transport and trade in bulbs, for example. But those innovations generally have a big influence on the landscape.
– Place large-scale innovations in the landscape.

Reuse

We live in a society that throws away a lot and uses many items just once, but that is changing quickly. Rubbish dumps used to grow bigger and bigger, but now they are surrounded by businesses that reuse the discarded items. Since raw materials are becoming more expensive, more things will be reused in the future. This applies to paper, wood, metal and plastic, and to buildings no longer used.
– Look for places, buildings or items where reuse plays a role.

Identity

What are your characteristics? Surely you ask yourself this now and again. For everybody is looking for their own identity. Not only people but also cities and regions are looking for their identity. In the past, the Bulb Region was the only place in the entire Netherlands where you could see fields in bloom. Now we have 'bulb regions' in other areas, in Noord-Holland and in Flevopolder for example.
– Determine what makes the Dune and Bulb Region and its people so special and strengthen that.

Housing

Since people are getting older and young people are leaving home earlier, the region must build more homes in the future. But what should the new homes look like? Just like in Groningen or Limburg? Then the entire Netherlands will look the same, and that would be boring. That's why there is increasing attention for 'region-specific' building. That means that the unique qualities of a building site are taken into consideration in the design of the homes. That makes the new neighbourhood more in harmony with the region.
– Let the characteristics of the region influence the design of the homes.

Empty bulb sheds

The traditional bulb sheds are disappearing from the landscape. Once there must have been more than a thousand of them in the region. Now they are losing their usefulness because today's climate installations and transport systems place different demands on the bulb shed. That is a pity, because it is precisely these sheds that tell us about the history of how the bulbs used to be dried and stored.

Archaeology

Many valuable things from our past lie buried in the ground. These items belong to our cultural history, but they are invisible. In the ground they are often better preserved (conserved) than they are after they have been dug up. For that, there must be some reason, such as a development plan. If the existence of valuable remains is suspected on a building site, then archaeological research is first conducted. It is precisely during development procedures that we often discover whether something special lies buried in the ground.

Untidy landscape

Previously, tourists drove in busses and cars through the wonderful bulb landscape when it was in bloom. Fifty years ago the Keukenhof came into being as a centre within the area. Now people come to Keukenhof only, and no longer drive through the landscape. Many bulb farmers therefore never consider whether the landscape where the bulbs are cultivated is interesting for tourists. They are largely concerned with the production of bulbs and erect bigger and bigger sheds in the landscape that obstruct the view of the bulb fields.

Unexpected influence

Some things happen very unexpectedly and have a huge influence that nobody could have predicted. What would happen to the region if a plane crashed there, or if the Netherlands won the World Cup? What does an unexpected event do to people and affect how they view their surroundings?

Rubbish

Archaeologists usually jump for joy when they discover a rubbish dump from the Middle Ages or Roman times. You can learn a lot about our history on a rubbish dump, certainly if it's more than fifty years old. Rubbish is the best way to learn about history. And that is no different with more recent mounds of rubbish. You can practice 'recent archaeology' not only on rubbish dumps but also in other places in the landscape.

Hybridization

Practising cultural planning is a bit like hybridization, or upgrading, which is what the bulb farmers do. They combine the best qualities of a flower to improve and renew it. And cultural planning is about continuing the development of landscape and cultural-historical qualities based on existing qualities. Nonetheless, it seems that the mentality of hybridization is absent in the region when it comes to spatial planning. It appears to be too difficult to combine existing (old) qualities with new possibilities.

BULB

the dunes for creating embankments in such places as Amsterdam. In fact, the landscape to which people are so attached represents the original one in 'ruined' form, but they nevertheless regard just that landscape as original. For that matter, no one is advocating redepositing a thick layer of sand on the bulb soil for cultivating beachgrass, although an extremely valid historical legitimation could be formulated for doing so.

Bulb cultivation, as well, supplied numerous remnants. For example, the typology of the bulb shed with its characteristic windows and doors for natural ventilation, whose creation was due to climatic requirements for storing the fragile bulb plants for flowers. The relevant requirements were determined within the limiting prerequisites of the time. As a result of the development of machines which could control the climate in a far more adequate manner in large metal halls, these sheds lost their function. Now that climate control is no longer a generator of heritage here, the introduction into the landscape of exchangeable industrial halls could take over that function. At the same time, the locations of, and space in, the old sheds are important elements which could lead to their effective re-use. Both of these remnants were translated into a competition. The task description entitled 'The desired Landscape' invited novel solutions for the introduction of large closed industrial premises to the open landscape.

Publication *Geest en Grond*. Design Kummer & Herrman. Photo: Dieuwertje Komen

culturele planologie in de duin- en bollenstreek

geest en grond

SOUL AND SOIL

SOUL AND SOIL. CULTURAL SPATIAL PLANNING IN THE DUNE AND BULB REGION commenced in January 2003 with a survey. The region was inventoried with an open mind, without biases or scientific intentions: if you like, an expedition with a clearly uncertain future, but which started with a clear objective in mind: finding remnants which can have meaning for future spatial developments. We discovered prominent remnants, which confirmed what we had already thought, but also found hardly perceptible ones, which stimulated curiosity or which embodied the promise of important finds. A number were submitted to more detailed research by experts. Other remnants could be translated into concrete competition assignments, which became the focus of the second phase of this project. The process of investigating and deploying cultural heritage is not concerned with the question whether to protect relicts of the past, but rather, is based on the refreshing effect that cultural heritage can have on the constantly changing spatial planning of an area. **SOUL AND SOIL** has brought qualities to light which could play a guiding, identity-giving or, indeed, development-hampering role.

The project revealed how bulb cultivation accounts for both the quality of the landscape and the bottlenecks it contains. The spatial situation in the Dune and Bulb Region is determined by the tension between, on the one hand, the desire to maintain the typical open landscape generated by bulb cultivation and, on the other, developments which are indispensable for keeping bulb cultivation economically profitable.

Against the current of developments, there is a clear desire to maintain the original landscape, a landscape which, incidentally, has only existed in its present form for some 150 years, and came about by excavating sand in

The task description, **BULB & BREAKFAST,** invited designs for a lodging facility in a bulb shed.

In addition, the discovery that thrift and re-use, not supposed profligacy, are what lie behind the internationally renowned Bloemencorso flower pageant, came as a surprise. Flowers are actually the waste product of bulb cultivation. Thus, *thrift* was the original inspiration for a creative form of processing waste, namely decorating wagons with it and having it paraded to the point of wilting through the entire region.

Acknowledgements

BULB was developed by Bureau Venhuizen in 2005/2006 for Erfgoed Zuid-Holland, and was based on the project, **SOUL AND SOIL,** cultural spatial planning in the Dune and Bulb Region. The website was made possible in part thanks to a subsidy from the Province of Zuid-Holland, the Belvedere project subsidy scheme of the Netherlands Architecture Fund, and the Prins Bernhard Cultuurfonds.

Concept management: Bureau Venhuizen – Hans Venhuizen, Mariëtte Maaskant, Margit Schuster.
Website and map design: Antenna-Men – Yvo Zijlstra and Marcel van der Zwet
Editors: Marieke Berkers, Onno Helleman and Marc Laman (Erfgoedhuis Zuid-Holland), Marleen van Ooststroom (intern), Karin Tabacnik, Francien van Westrenen, Afshan Ayar.
Thanks to: Peter Sevens, Willem Venhuizen, Anne Sevens, Hanne Hagenaars, Marjan Teunissen, Thea de Langen, Rob van Iterson (Hoogheemraadschap Rijnland).

Image on previous page: Preparations for the annual flower parade. Photo: Dieuwertje Komen

BULB

BULB SHED The traditional bulb sheds are obsolete quickly. Paint them on time or else they'll rot away.

SAND LIZARD You are a sand lizard and you can prevent the construction of houses by digging tunnels in the right places and sticking your head above ground.

COLOURFUL BULB FIELDS The brightly coloured flowers in particular are impressive. Change the colour of the fields until you think they are most beautiful.

BULB LAB The historical bulb laboratory is threatened with demolition. Chase the demolition machines away by throwing bulbs at them.

DELFWEG The agricultural landscape is increasingly turning into an untidy business park. Tidy it up.

KEUKENHOF The Keukenhof flower garden is threatened by the advancing bulbs. Keep the park free of large-scale bulb-growing.

KEROSINE CONTOUR More and more houses are being built, unless the aeroplanes fly over really low.

LOOK AFTER YOUR GUESTS You have visitors in your Bulb & Breakfast. Before sunrise, work out what you need for breakfast, otherwise the tourists will walk away moaning.

REUSE Collect all sorts of rubbish with which you can build wonderful things and even bring history back to life.

206

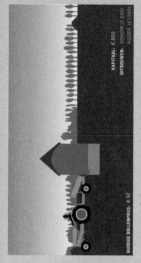

NIX VERSTEHEN A Polish and a Dutch worker sitting at a table and trying to understand each other's language. Every time they guess the meaning of a word correctly they drink a glass.

Als het nog zo klein,
in Warmond wil ik zijn.
Daar aan de Leede is het mooi
Daar wonen is zo . . . . .

Binnen: 1   zakgeld: € 2832000

TOLL BRIDGE Pensioners standing in front of the historical bridge in Warmond. They have to fill in the missing words in the anthem to close the bridge, or else they end up in the canal.

MUSEUMCONSULENTSCHAP
Bij het Erfgoedhuis zijn een dietal museumconsulenten belast met de ondersteuning van de museale sector.

HERITAGE HOUSE A memory game of varied tasks for the Erfgoedhuis Zuid-Holland.

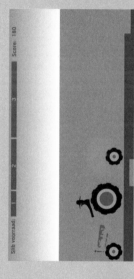

Silb voorraad: 1   2   3   Score: 180

SLUDGE Spread the polluted sludge evenly over the land.

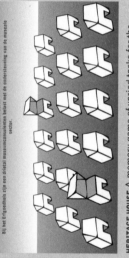

HUIDIGE BOLLENPRIJS: € 92

KAPITAAL: € 600
UITBOUWEN: SCHUUR (€ 600)
KELDER (€ 1200)

INVESTMENT Investment in the bulb sheds is dependent on the revenue from the bulbs. Increase your profit as much as possible with the current price of bulbs.

GEVANGEN 1   SCORE 10

FISH WRECK Lying off the coast is a shipwreck in which fish like to breed. If you guide them inside you can catch more later.

Francien van Westrenen
URBANISM GAME
The playful person in spatial planning

'New-Babylonians play a game of their own creation, against a back-drop they have designed themselves.'[1] About fifty years ago, Constant Nieuwenhuys saw the playful person as the starting point for a new kind of urbanism that he researched and depicted in his New Babylon project. The condition for creating such a new kind of person was a living space where a decor based purely on function was replaced by a playing field of spatial experiences. This had not only a physical influence on the person, but more importantly, a mental one. The change in lifestyle and needs of that person would concurrently also manifest itself in urbanism and architecture, because, according to Constant, when the people change, so does their environment. How that would happen, and under which circumstances, he really didn't know.[2] Constant studied the relationship between culture and urbanism, between the playful person and his environment. That relationship is also at the core of this book about Hans Venhuizen's work.

The game is an important element in many of the projects that Hans Venhuizen develops. The structure of a game – with its field, its goal and its rules – is closely related to the way he tries to express the process of spatial planning and cohabitation. Within that process, he distinguishes between the ambitions and phenomena that together form a matrix within which the situation that must or will change can be described. In game terms: the given situation (described using ambitions and phenomena) creates the playing field, the goal is almost always the design of the commission (the actual task in the given situation), and the rules can in fact be reduced to the terms 'continuism' and 'opportunism.' This first term relates to the idea that culture is part of the way in which space is created within the time and place of operation. In reducing this mode of creation to rules and then applying them, culture remains central to the form of future space. According to Venhuizen, one needs an 'opportimistic' eye to see this: to be open, curious, strategic, un-disciplinary, opportunistic and optimistic towards the qualities and singularities present in a place and connect them with the future task so as to allow new qualities to emerge.

Venhuizen's games are not that easy to grasp. They have a formal structure and a fixed form, come with an array of rules and require concentration from the players. They are a simulation of complex reality, and offer a space within which to debate complicated issues while still having fun. The form of the game allows Venhuizen to involve various groups – from professionals to lay people – in the process of spatial planning and cohabitation. When a game is a part of a spatial process, the players contribute to the content and

1
Mark Wigley, *Constant's New Babylon. The hyper-architecture of desire*, Rotterdam 1998.

2
Anna Tilroe, 'Miskend ben ik zeker', *NRC Handelsblad*, January 16, 2004.

form of the future spatial situation. The 'playful person' is thus an important factor in the conception and work involved in spatial planning. This led to the title, *Game Urbanism*: a book about the culture of spatial planning, showing the importance of the game in the design of 'urbanization'. The reverse title, *Urbanism Game*, depicts a game about spatial planning, coupled with the players of that game. And that is what this article is all about.

To explain the game of spatial planning, Hans Venhuizen and I talked with five players in the field: historian Jan Kolen (professor at the VU Amsterdam), cultural planner Bert van Meggelen (Bureau Maatwerk), sociologist Willem Schinkel (Erasmus University Rotterdam), urbanist Hilde Blank (director of BVR), and political geographer Martijn Duineveld (Wageningen University). These discussions, covering subjects such as culture, citizen involvement, planning, framing, position and strategy, lay the foundation for the first part of this article about the *Urbanism Game*. What follows in part two, *Urbanism Gamers*, covers the (future) players of the game. The third part describes the results: the creation of *Game Urbanism*.

URBANISM GAME

A spatial situation, for example a town with inhabitants, creates the playing field of the Urbanism Game, with the goal of making a settlement possible and attractive in the field, using rules determined by planning and urbanism. To play the game well, we need a process in which strategy and position are set. Culture offers a point of connection to give the game content. And finally, fluency in various languages and the use of images are of great importance to communications among players.

Field of play
From afar, the field of play seems well organized and under control with fenced off and outlined green areas, power districts, zones of opportunity and danger, creative hotspots and problem areas. That is all simply an illusion of course; the city is not geographically flat. Urban space is hybrid and complex and also experienced mentally. To understand a city, you have to be on the street. An incredible diversity of residents inhabits a city, each one with a different vision of the city depending on where and how they live. Sociologist Willem Schinkel suggests that there is a strong correlation between citizenship and spatial planning. He refers to neoliberal citizenship: everyone is responsible for his or her own living environment and is 'allowed to participate' in decision-making. This focus on participation is in sharp contrast with the situation of the last fifty years when politics took pity on public space. It is obvious for example in security issues; citizens are now asked to become the eyes and ears of society in order to control irregularities. Schinkel calls this a fake participation: citizens lack the formal powers of authority to enforce different behaviour.

Citizens are also increasingly consulted in spatial processes. They are asked all kinds of questions: Should this building stay? Should we build a tower for pigs? Which architect should design the municipal office building? What's the future of our region? Often this kind of participation is reduced to a consultation without a clear goal for its results. According to cultural planner Bert van Meggelen, it creates distrust for spatial planners, with their jargon and their failure to appreciate the opinions of citizens.

Whichever way he looks at it, Van Meggelen sees no infrastructure to accommodate independently-minded citizens adequately.

Van Meggelen also feels that the individualization of citizenship has created a society of minorities that traditional urbanism has no instruments to cope with. Citizens are becoming more independent and are accustomed to having influence and being in a position to take initiative and to shape their own home or environment, yet in practice they often lose out to technocratic planners. On the other hand, political geographer Martijn Duineveld sees dubious sides to the extreme 'belief' in citizens and their local knowledge. Quoting Frank Zappa, he says: 'Locals can be assholes too.' Citizens are often considered sacred in spatial processes, but when you study theses processes, you often see a lot of personal directions and most of all personal motives.

Goal

The goal of the Urbanism Game is really to organize the space for the best possible settlement of residents, businesses and amenities in such a way as to create urban quality. This means constantly reconsidering different interests, such as commercial activities, houses, green areas, public spaces, infrastructure, recreational facilities, culture or entertainment.

For a long time, economy was always the motor behind urban development, and it is still often the case. A city is sometimes almost a business that wants to distinguish itself in the competition with other cities to attract the most, the richest and the best clients – i.e. businesses and inhabitants. Urban planning and architecture are the ideal instruments to cement that urban identity, for example with an iconic building or a large-scale area development. Culture is also gaining in importance, which sometimes leads to the focus turning to the creation of new cultural facilities rather than on the use of existing cultural qualities in the city. The race towards the title of Cultural Capital of Europe is one of the causes of this trend, according to Schinkel. All kinds of investments are made, mostly superficially, to bring in a nomination, and lead to cities grabbing at grotesque gestures with fast effects and vast marketing campaigns, while subtle interventions on a smaller scale might have a much more lasting effect on residents.

Rules

There is a great contrast between the world of top-down planning, urbanism and spatial planning on the one hand and autonomous experience, knowledge and individuality on the other. It is incredibly difficult to bring the two together, remarks urbanist Hilde Blank. They are worlds that neither know each other nor speak each other's language. The former is driven by the long-term and the abstract, while the latter is concerned with the here and now and is directly connected with a place. There is a lot more time spent on the former, while there is much more need for the latter. The tradition of planning in the Netherlands is pragmatic and instrumental, suggests historian Jan Kolen. To break through, we must 'go beyond feasibility, legalization, measurability, control issues and look towards actual movements, wishes, actions and desires of people', says Martijn Duineveld. That requires most of all letting go of the pragmatic design or planning position, because terms such as desires and movements are not easily translated one to one into a design. Moreover, the rules need to be re-examined, not to throw the whole legal basis of planning overboard, but to search for new applications that work with developments such as temporariness, an economic

211

crisis, sustainability and citizen participation. The way in which rules are currently applied often shuts processes down, while they should actually create freedom.

Strategy, position en process
Without a feeling for strategy, it is difficult to operate within spatial planning. The strategy determines the position within the process of change. In order to be able to direct the process, Hilde Blank considers it necessary to speak to as many people as possible, so as to formulate the question more sharply, to be alert to all the functional elements, to strengthen the individuality of the story, to ensure that it remains the story of the place at the same time, and to learn the different languages needed to ensure good communication between the various parties. Leadership involvement and mutual trust are indispensable to the process for Blank: 'Ask leaders to participate in thinking and to be ready to accept a different result, commit yourself to showing and developing a real interest in an area, invest in foundations and ownership, organize fun, and have an eye for people without knowledge of urban planning.'

Culture
Planning is a cultural act, at least if you start with the definition that culture is constantly developing in the practice itself, as in a continuous process. Jan Kolen refers to the phenomenology that uses this notion: culture immediately occurs in the practice of doing – in the space of here and now. Within this notion, time is a quality in which new things can come into being. Kolen considers this to be a completely different position to the pragmatic, anti-intellectual concept of time applied by most planners. In spatial processes that often last years, time is most often seen as a hurdle to be overcome. Time to think, to let ideas ripen, to come back on an earlier decision, has no place in current planning practice. In this practice, culture is also considered as a thing apart, a lone paragraph in the structural vision, and an obligation to be ticked off, instead of an integral part of the process of change. Culture must also primarily be something positive, something fun; but Kolen sees no space for a loaded heritage, stories that speak of a dark past or the culture of minorities. He sees this unidimensional concept of culture and the denial of its diversity as having a great impact on the way in which we plan space and develop cities.

Bringing in culture also begs the question of which notion of culture is right, or which culture should lead in a certain development. Determining the identity of culture is, according to Martijn Duineveld, 'a defensive fight, fought by a number of white baby boomers wanting to use their position to cement their identity once and for all in a canon'. They are overtaken left and right by technology: the iPhone and *augmented reality* (enhanced interactive reality, for example in the form of extra layers of information) will determine which culture or history is important in a particular place. And then it is only about where you direct your iPhone and who has added information about that place. Almost all information about a particular place – appealing, unappealing, from before till now – is available to anyone; and not only available, but also open to anyone's influence. In connection to this, Jan Kolen refers to the role the past already plays in the lives of many people. He brings in the ideas of American scientist Angela Landsberg, whose book *Prosthetic Memory* speaks of 'transferential spaces'. The relationship of the past is becoming more and more personal, suggests Landsberg. That requires a high quality of staging to create an image in living colour, which allows you to feel part of a past that you took a part in yourself. The result of this extreme identification is that people start to make their own history. The past is then not just a representation of a situation, but something that you can exert some influence over. In short, culture and history are not just created from the top down, but also develop from the bottom up.

In order to give culture a role of importance, Hilde Blank finds that a parallel process is best. This process is coupled with a flexible planning process, flexible in the sense that there is space for change in the course of time, for example as a result of the cultural process. There must be a form for the interaction between both processes. A parallel process offers the freedom to figure things out in a way that is free from everyday planning reality by, for example, bringing in an artist. Art can bring out unexpected qualities, uncover other dimensions in the larger process, initiate another way of looking and seeing and thus stimulate a more fundamental delibera-tion of what to do with a particular place. Art can enrich the process in this manner, not per se with 'nice' but certainly with 'unique' insights.

Bert van Meggelen believes that there are four levels on which cultural interventions in spatial planning can be measured. First of all, culture as a subsection of art and culture: bringing culture in creates an artistic product that can be considered a work of art. Second, as a cultural dimension of something else, for example mobility or food, thereby throwing another light on the task. Or third culture as the yeast and sourdough of the urban society: tasteless in and of itself, but that which makes something else rise, makes it light, full and serious. Finally, culture as the salt of the urban slop, giving it some taste. According to Van Meggelen, the most successful interventions have something of all four: working as a catalyst, touching on another sector and breaking something open, making things tastier, and creating an artistic product.

Language and image
Language and image are two instruments not to be underestimated in spatial planning. Both are essential in translating between the spatial and the non-spatial world. Martijn Duineveld feels the relationship between language and politics is very sensitive, citing Maarten Hajer: 'words matter in politics and planning'. In the world of planning, certain words such as pig tower, acid rain or cluttering come about more or less by accident. They are also created intentionally and used as instruments: a good slogan or title can give a process identity, making it easier to go along with. One step further is the terrain of framing. The way you frame the world determines how you think about it and what kind of reactions you have. Whether you look at spatial planning with the 'Netherlands is full' frame or with the 'Netherlands is part of Europe' frame makes a big difference. The frame therefore not only constructs new ways of thinking about the world, but also has an effect on how we then deal with it. Just as language consciously creates perspectives, images too can be con-vincing and manipulative. A good image, a good depiction of an idea or design in a visualization or map, can give people insight into how things will look. Visualizations are becoming more and more realistic. Bright 3D animations allow future residents to wander among and even inside build-ings. But no matter how realistic these kinds of visualizations seem, they remain simulations and often paint a rosier image than reality and tend moreover to stick definitively in people's minds.

213

Tension

All the interviewees point on the one hand to how the situation is at present, but then also to the places gathering tension: where citizens are given more responsibility but the facilities do not exist to take them seriously, where a desired, imagined outcome rather than everyday reality takes a leading role, where pragmatism, rules and legalization gain the upper hand on experience, expertise and the desires of users and residents, where diversity of culture is not seen as a strength any more but a weakness, where time is cursed and not used, where protecting personal positions costs more energy than carrying the project out, where so much nuance in language is lost that the frame starts to take on a life of its own, where disparate disciplines win out over an integral approach. And that does not even cover the content of spatial assignments such as identity, population shrinkage, mobility, sustainability, health and safety. In short, a lot more is required from the players to bring the game to a good conclusion. It throws down a challenge to create other instruments and abilities, to take a different approach to the questions at hand and to find new rules. It actually asks for a completely new type of player, whose novel approach can play (out) the Urbanism Game.

URBANISM GAMERS

At the moment, society is shifting from being hierarchically ordered and organized to relying more on networks and horizontal relationships. This development creates a new type of 'player' in society who can also have an influence on the way we think about and design the space around us. And who is in a position to play this game much better.

Participation as a leading principle

Do-it-yourself and organize-it-yourself: those wanting to exercise some influence themselves, and thereby also find ways to do it, will have a great influence on society, suggests the British innovation specialist Charles Leadbeater. According to him, we are witnessing a fundamental change in the relationship between producer and consumer: 'In a short space of time, participation on a large scale has become more important than mass consumption. We want to become players and co-creators ourselves, not simply observers or passive consumers. New technology makes it possible for everyone to let his or her voice be heard. People want to share things with others, they want to be where the action is, they want acknowledgement for what they know and what they do.' Leadbeater speaks of the *with* economy, in which you do something with others, in contrast to the old *to* or *for* economy, in which you decide for others. The principle of *user-generated content* is not only behind YouTube but also many video game productions. The space that caters to this behaviour is the Internet, and more specifically online networking made up of more equal social connections. It creates new ways of organizing ourselves: horizontally, not hierarchically. You don't need to be sitting in an organization to get organized. Participation is, according to Leadbeater, the new leading principle and it has serious implications for businesses that have to learn new ways to deal with their clients – and with their employees. [3]

Today's 'playful person' shares, connects and combines knowledge, needs to keep constantly abreast of new possibilities and applications, takes part in many social networks, searches opportunistically for useful information, throws away what doesn't fit the bill, plays on what seems

3
Tracy Metz, 'Wij willen allemaal spelers zijn, geen toeschouwers', *NRC Handelsblad*, June 6, 2008.

important, doesn't believe in 'game over', learns from mistakes and keeps trying until the game is won. The new player wants to exert influence on how things are done, and wants to be able to change the outcome. The spectator has become a participant.

The playing style of this new type of player is already to be seen in people around you, from writers to politicians, from economists to architects, mostly in young people, but also in older ones and sometimes even in dead ones who were before their time, and maybe also in yourself. It is a playing style that we will all increasingly be faced with. Translated in terms of spatial planning, you can ask whether this new playing style offers any possibilities, or even shows the necessity to deal differently with the tensions mentioned here above. And if so, how would we describe this new type of player?

Entrepreneur

Luigi Ferrara, director of the leading experimental Institute without Boundaries (Toronto, Canada), sees a new kind of designer coming up, which he names the entrepreneur.[4] These designers start with questioning and redefining the task, then research possible solutions and ways to bring them about. Ferrara sees the entrepreneur emerging among designers but does not think it is reserved only for them. You can consider this style of play as the result of the societal developments sketched out by Leadbeater, and also as the answer to the tensions in spatial planning as described by the experts.

In the broadest description, entrepreneurs are those who undertake and connect. They create value by offering a product or service, or by fill-ing a gap in the market. By operating cleverly and taking risks, they try to bring about a development that changes existing interactions. Economists differentiate between kinds of entrepreneurs, one of which is the social en-trepreneur. This kind's main objective is to create social value by improving goods and services. This improvement must be for the good of society itself. Entrepreneurs in spatial planning are proactive and invested in society. They research the processes that are at the foundation of the task and try to understand and influence the interaction between people and space and to offer an optimistic and holistic vision of the issues. They strive to win, which in their case means finding a solution. Coincidence and time are important factors, as well as co-operation with others or so-called amateurs in the field who are actively involved in the project. Playing – puzzling over what comes up, shifting between thinking and doing, and stimulating interaction – is an important element in their working philosophy. And finally, entrepre-neurs are good translators: they have the skills to translate the qualities of one world into the wishes of another.

You can also see the playing style of the entrepreneur as an answer to the tensions in spatial planning that ask for a different approach to the questions at hand. This approach researches and questions, strives for meaningful participation, is not stuck but moves with changes, places the creation of value in the centre, organizes freedom, focuses on the answer, offers an interdisciplinary approach, and can simultaneously think and negotiate. This approach makes culture an integral part of spatial develop-ments: culture in the sense of heritage, art, architecture and mentality, but also the culture of a place in the meaning of individuality and the creation of history. In this book, this new approach to spatial planning will be labelled Game Urbanism, and Hans Venhuizen's practice is one example of it.

4
Luigi Ferrara (director of the Institute without Boundaries), 'The power of entrepreneur-ship', lecture in Z33, Hasselt, December 9, 2009.

The key to renewal in the practice of spatial planning lies with our cultural approach to space, one that starts with the complexity of the task. The game can be of great value in developing this approach.

In his *Homo Ludens* (1938), Johan Huizinga wrote that culture essentially comes from a game: a person is and must be a player. More recently, Pat Kane published *The Play Ethic* (2004), a plea for a playful society; according to him, play leads to creativity, continuous learning and experiment. In *Design and Politics* (2009), Henk Ovink asks for the development of reflective abilities, to learn from our mistakes: 'Reflection is essentially a form of seduction, it can persuade you to adopt new insights, to change your perspectives.' He believes it is urgently necessary in the practice of spatial planning to think, test and undertake simultaneously.[5] Hans Venhuizen also underlines the necessity to 'make believe' in spatial processes, whereby both play and seriousness are present. He believes that the core of every process of change lies in the pleasure of the connectedness between seriousness and play. 'Play has the capacity to give you insight into the situation in transition that goes far beyond your own interest and awareness.'

The game acts as a simulation of complex reality and offers the opportunity to practice and make mistakes. It gives a form to participation and organizes interaction; it gives citizens a role in spatial planning by making them part of the development before them. They become, as it were, part of the culture that gives shape to the space, whereby the process of spatial planning also becomes more cultural. The game creates a mutual experience without covering up differences. It generates ideas, gives information and, above all, provides playfulness. Games are, after all, accessible and horizontal, they have clear-cut rules that apply to everyone and each player has, in principle, the same chances of winning. The game takes its shape in the playing, which means that it can change under the influence of its players. These make up the space of the game and vice versa, the new space also creates new players.

We find ourselves in the middle of a process of renewal in which spatial and societal developments ask for new abilities and, conversely, the development of new abilities has an influence on spatial and societal developments. In short, where people and their environment come into a new kind of relationship.

5
Erik Frijters and Olv Klijn, '"Spatial planning is everything at once". Interview with Henk Ovink', *Ontwerp en politiek* no. 1 (2009), pp 333-349, p 347.

Francien van Westrenen has been producing architectural events at Stroom The Hague, centre for art and architecture, since 2007. The programme comprises exhibitions, publications, debates and projects that focus on an interdisciplinary, cultural approach to the urban environment. Prior to that she worked for four years at Bureau Venhuizen on projects that included **THE MAKING OF MHEENPARK, SOUL AND SOIL, WAPLA** and **DES BEEMSTERS**.

LIST OF PROJECTS

1992

'Een ruimtelijke ordening schaal 1:60', exhibition in collaboration with Marcel Smink at the Hooghuis, Arnhem.

Stichting L,v (Locus *Velocitas*) established with Marcel Smink and Frank Hemeltjen.

1993

'Locus *Velocitas*', concept and organization of a group exhibition at the GEWAB-building in Arnhem, featuring Raoul Bunschoten, John Körmeling, Wim Nijenhuis and others. Publication.

Publication: H. Venhuizen, *Verpretparking*, Arnhem 1993. Publication of office's work, edited and produced by the office with the assistance of Heleen Lamers and Barbara Mayreder.

1994

'Kadaster', concept and organization of a group exhibition in Utrecht, featuring Frank Havermans, Rob Groot Zevert, Carolina Agelink and others. Pamphlet.

'Meeneemstad', exhibition at Motta, Eindhoven, in collaboration with Frank Hemeltjen and Marcel Smink. Pamphlet.

'De Arnhemse School. 25 jaar monumentale kunst', participant in a group exhibition in Arnhem alongside Bas Maters, Wim Korvinus, Jan van Ijzendoorn and others. Publication: M. Fritz-Jobse and Ineke Middag (eds), *De Arnhemse School: 25 jaar monumentale kunst*, Arnhem (Hogeschool voor de kunsten) 1994.

1995

'Potsdam, Vorschläge zur Stadtgestaltung', participation in event as part of 'Eutopia', Potsdam, Germany. Featuring Willem de Ridder, Geert van Tijn and Büro für ungewöhnliche Massnahmen.

Publication: *Der Opportimist*, Potsdam 1995. German-language publication about the office's work, edited and produced by the office with the assistance of Wigger Bierma and Volker Oelschläger.

1996

Publication: H. Venhuizen, 'U bevindt zich niet hier', in: Jacqueline Tellinga and Arjen Mulder (eds), *L'Europe à grande vitesse*, Rotterdam/Amsterdam 1996 (NAi Publishers/Fonds BKVB), pp 66-77. Authors included Vincent van Rossem, Joost Schrijnen and Maike van Stiphout.

'2 x 5 ungefragte Vorschläge zur Stadtgestaltung', exhibition at Galerie im Staudenhof, Potsdam, Germany. In collaboration with Marcel Smink.

'Urbs Simu Lipsk' voor 'LebenLeben', participation in group exhibition in the Messehaus Petershof, Leipzig, Germany. Catalogue.

1997

'Het zelfkarterend landschap', participation in a group exhibition within the framework of 'Benaderingen', NBKS, Breda. Participants included Sjaak Langenberg, Mirjam de Zeeuw and QS Serafijn. Publication.

'Planologische Hallucinaties', participation in a group exhibition at the Netherlands Architecture Institute, Rotterdam. Participants included Justin Bennett, Marinus Boezem and Buro Schie.

1998

''t luie End', participation in a group exhibition at the Ω Case Study House, Utrecht.

'Villa Horizon' and 'Villa Dijkweg', proposals for the project 'Undercover. New possibilities for 'attic and basement' in new suburban homes Stichting Locus Velocitas/Stichting Undercover, Arnhem. Travelling group exhibition to Groningen, Eindhoven, Delft and other places. Participants included Wim van den Bergh, Gijs Wallis de Vries and Lars Spuybroek. Publication: A. Habets, F. Sturkenboom and J-P. Kerstens (eds), *Undercover. Over de terugkeer van zolders en kelders in de hedendaagse architectuur,* Nijmegen 1998 (SUN).

'The art of settling', research project 'Kunst en ruimtelijke ordening' at Gouda, commissioned by the Municipality of Gouda and the Province of Zuid-Holland. Publication: H. Venhuizen (ed.), *De Kunst van het Vestigen*, Gouda 1998. Published by the office. Contributors included Bart Lootsma, NL Architects and Paul Meurs.

'Amsterdam Public Transport Safari', manifestation at the Veemvloer, Amsterdam.

1999

'Parquet Garden', design and construction of a garden for Amarant Tilburg, an institute for the mentally handicapped. Commissioned by the Praktijkbureau Amsterdam/Stichting Amarant, Tilburg. With the assistance of Albert Koolma, Margit Schuster, Don van Grunsven, Mariska Noordik, Martine Herman and others. Pamphlet.

2000

'Amphibious Living', competition, project of implementation and exhibition as a follow-up to the project 'De Kunst van het Vestigen' (Hans Venhuizen, Gouda 1998). Commissioned by Kunstgebouw and the Province of Zuid-Holland. With the assistance of Maureen Timmermans, Irmin Eggens, Caroline Wolf, ZEE, Parthesius Vormgeving and others. Publication: H. Venhuizen (ed.), *Amfibisch Wonen/Amphibious Living*, Rotterdam 2000 (NAi Publishers).

'Commitment. Een keuze uit drie jaar Fonds BKVB', participation in a group exhibition in Las Palmas, Rotterdam. Publication.

2000-2002

'The discovery of the Flood Plain Model', concept and organization of the research project 'Kunst en ruimtelijke ordening'. Commissioned by the Province of Gelderland and Stichting van Weurt tot Deest, Beuningen. With the assistance of Maureen Timmermans, Hilde de Bruijn, Inge Hoonte and Margot Lieftinck and others. Contributors included Heitor Frugoli Junior, Sjaak Langenberg and 2012Architecten. Publication.

2001

'Nieuw Erfgoed', participatory design project in Winssen, Gelderland. In collaboration with the residents, administrators and designers. Commissioned by the municipality of Beuningen. With the assistance of Max Daniel, Steven Venhuizen, Marieke Berkers, Beeldleveranciers, Caroline Wolf and others. Pamphlet.

'Squaresaver', project proposal for 'Kunst in de publieke ruimte' in Amsterdam. With the assistance of Marleen Oud, Olivier Scheffer and others. Commissioned by the Amsterdams Fonds voor de Kunst (not built).

Publication: H. Venhuizen (ed.), *Shared authorship, conceptmanagement, art and urbanism*, Rotterdam 2001. Publication about the office's work, produced by the office. With the assistance of Wigger Bierma, Anniek Brattinga and Margit Schuster.

'Archilab', participation in a group exhibition and architecture congress, Orléans, France. Publication.

'Ort.Zukunft', workshop within the framework of Stadtumbau-Programma in East Germany, Bauhaus Dessau, Germany. Other participants included Raumlaborberlin, Phillip Oswalt and Büro für Spaziergangsforschung. Pamphlet.

218

'Geschiedenis opdoen', master plan for 'Kunst in de publieke ruimte' in Nieuwegein. Commissioned by the Municipality of Nieuwegein. Pamphlet.

2001–2002

'The phenomenal road', concept development. Commissioned by Rijkswaterstaat and SKOR. With contributions by Boris Sieverts, Hans van Houwelingen, Paul Meurs and The Good Guys. With the assistance of Caroline Wolf, Johanne Luhmann, Marieke Berkers and others. Pamphlet.

2001

'RESERVE', creation and supervision of master plan for 'Kunst in de publieke ruimte' in Wateringen. Commissioned by the municipality of Wateringen and Kunstgebouw. Pamphlet.

2002

'The Making Of... Marzahn', spatial design project on the basis of the concept development game The Making Of. In collaboration with the residents, administrators and designers. Concept and implementation commissioned by the city district Marzahn-Hellersdorf, Berlin. With the assistance of Caroline Wolf. Pamphlet.

2002–2003

'The Making Of... Mheenpark', spatial design project on the basis of the concept development game The Making Of. In collaboration with the residents, administrators and designers. Concept and implementation commissioned by the municipality of Apeldoorn. With the assistance of Francien van Westrenen, Dieuwertje Komen, Inge Hoonte, Martin Leclercq and others. Pamphlet.

2002–2004

'Soul and Soil', cultural planning in the Dune and Bulb Region. Concept management and organization of the research project 'Soul and Soil'. Commissioned by the Erfgoedhuis Zuid-Holland. With the assistance of Onno Helleman, Inge Hoonte, Francien van Westrenen, Mariëtte Maaskant, Isabel van der Zande, and others; design publication: Kummer & Herrman.
Publication: H. Venhuizen (ed.), Geest en Grond, Rotterdam 2004. Produced by the office. Contributors included Paul Meurs, Krijn Giezen, Tom Frantzen, Jennifer Petterson, BAVO (Gideon Boie and Matthias Pauwels), Catherine Visser, DaF-architecten. Results of the competition 'Bulb & Breakfast', 'Het gewenste landschap' and 'Nieuw Erfgoed'. Follow-up studies with Artgineering, Delft University of Technology, 'The Dutch Bulbs' prize winners and others, and

comments from Annemiek Rijckenberg, Zef Hemel, and others.

Publication: H. Venhuizen, 'Te late schaarste', in: H. Geerlings and G. Peeters (ed.), Mobiliteit als uitdaging: Een integrale benadering, Rotterdam 2002 (010 Publishers), pp 199-203.

2003

'WAPLA, the art of car washing', concept management of the project. Kunstenaars, designers and architects design car washes. Commissioned by the City of Utrecht/Bureau BEYOND. Including BAR, Frank de Bruijn, Marcel Schmalgemeijer and Kaptein Roodnat. With the assistance of Francien van Westrenen, Dieuwertje Komen, Felix Janssens and others. Pamphlet.

Jury member in 'Hotel Neustadt', project about the shrinking city, Raumlaborberlin for Thalia Theater, Halle, Germany. Manifestation and publication.

'Heemskerk: Wo ist der Bahnhof', research project. Commissioned by the Province of Noord-Holland and the Municipality of Heemskerk. With the assistance of Isabel van der Zande.

2004

'Schrumpfende Stadt. Stassfurt', Bauhaus Dessau, Germany. Workshop and manifestation.

Publication: H. Venhuizen, 'Alles wird gut', in: C. Wagenaar (ed.), Ideals in Concrete: Exploring Central and Eastern Europe, Rotterdam/ Amsterdam 2004 (NAi Publishers/Fonds BKVB), pp 92-97. Authors included Anna Tilroe, Vincent van Rossem and Wies Sanders.

2004–2006

'Doing-as-if', design and realization of a playground. Commissioned by the City of Hilversum and the Province of Noord-Holland. With the assistance of Olivier Scheffer, Joost Volkers, Margit Schuster, Wigger Bierma and others.
Various articles in NRC Handelsblad, Architecture in the Netherlands: Yearbook 2006/2007, Nederlandse designprijzen 2007, and more.

2005

'Recreatie actueel', definition of a competition programme about cultural planning for the Province of Noord-Holland. With the assistance of Francien van Westrenen and Gerke Veenboer.

Publication: H. Venhuizen, 'Tippelroute', in: B. Post (ed.), Lof der Onzin, Amsterdam 2005 (Uitgeverij Balans), p 181.

2005–2006

'LIMES, the future of history', concept development and implementation of a design project about the role of cultural history in future spatial development. Commissioned by the Projectbureau Belvedere and The Netherlands Architecture Fund. With the assistance of Francien van Westrenen, Dieuwertje Komen, Wigger Bierma and others. Publication: H. Venhuizen (ed.), Limes. De toekomst van de geschiedenis, Rotterdam 2005. Produced by the office. Contributors included Juurlink+Geluk landschapsarchitecten, Karres en Brands landschapsarchitecten and 1:1 Stadslandschappen.

'BULB', composition and production of an educational website about cultural history and spatial planning on the basis of the results of 'Soul and Soil'. Commissioned by the Erfgoedhuis Zuid-Holland, the Province of Zuid-Holland and the Belvedere (www.bulb-web.nl). With the assistance of Mariëtte Maaskant, Margit Schuster, Antenna-Men and others.

2005–2010

'Des Beemsters I and II' and Bureau Des Beemsters, creation and implementation of a future vision about the role of the UNESCO World Heritage in the future spatial planning of the Beemster. Project commissioned by the Province of Noord-Holland and Milieufederatie Noord-Holland (I and II) and the Municipality of Beemster. With the assistance of Francien van Westrenen, Dieuwertje Komen, Piet Snellaars and others. In collaboration with Marinke Steenhuis, Paul Meurs, Patrick McCabe and the Municipality of Beemster (Harry Roenhorst and Han Hefting among others).

2006

Publication: H. Venhuizen and M. Schuster (eds.), Urbaan Glutamaat, Rotterdam/Xiamen 2006. Publication about urban developments in China, published by the office during a stay at the Chinese European Art Centre in Xiamen.

Publication: H. Venhuizen, 'Culture based planning', in: World Architecture, E. Kögel (ed.), Beijing 2006, pp 78-89.

'De stad gaat altijd door', concept, compilation and realization of a Master course in urban planning for the Rotterdam Academy of Architecture. With the assistance of Francien van Westrenen and contributions from Rudy Stroink, Wies Sanders, Rients Dijkstra and others.

Publication: H. Venhuizen, 'Living on estate agents' water', in: TOPOS, Wageningen 2006, 57, pp 64-70.

Publication: H. Venhuizen, 'Je moet niet alles willen wat kan', in: S. Cusveller and L. Melis (eds), *Regionale identiteit*, Rotterdam/Amsterdam 2006 (NAi Publishers/SKOR), pp 144-147.

2006-2007

'Under Construction', concept and realization of the Archiprix study visit to Beijing and Shanghai, China. Commissioned by Hunter Douglas Rotterdam. With the assistance of Francien van Westrenen, Tanja Reith, Eduard Kögel and others. Pamphlet.

2007

'The Happy Crab', research into the reuse of a Midden-Delflands recreation area. In the framework of 'Case Study Krabbeplas', a project by SKOR, the City of Vlaardingen and Groenservice Zuid-Holland. With the assistance of Robin Kolleman, Minke Themans, Francien van Westrenen, Bert van Meggelen, Esther Didden and others. Contributors included Jacques Abelman, Rianne Makkink and Willemijn Lofvers.
Publication: H. Venhuizen and F. van Westrenen (eds),*The Happy Crab en andere voorstellen voor de toekomst van de Krabbeplas,* Rotterdam 2007. Produced by the office.

'Tesameheid in Autonia', proposal for the Laboratory of the interim. Project aimed at transforming theTransvaal district in The Hague. Commissioned by OpTrek. With the assistance of Brigitta van Weeren and others.

2008–2009

'Parquette Settlement Game' urbanization in co-creation. Part of the exhibition 'TEAMWORK. Een hedendaagse ontwerppraktijk' in Museum De Paviljoens, Almere. With the assistance of Mark van derWegen, Brigitta van Weeren, Erik-Jan Mans, Els Brouwer, Annemarie van den Berg and others.

'The Making Of', concept development and debate game at the Netherlands Architecture Institute, Rotterdam. Within the framework of the 'Make our Country' event programme. With the assistance of Observatorium, Netherlands Architecture Institute, Anneke Abhelakh, Leo van Loon and others.

'VEENBREED', project plan for the Venen area in the Green Heart. Commissioned by Centrum voor Beeldende Kunst (CBKU), Province of Utrecht.

'Guanxi Game', concept and design of a network game in China. In collaboration withTanja Reith and with the assistance

of Annemarie van den Berg, Francien van Westrenen and many others.

'Hoge Vucht, geschiedenis opdoen of om-katten', research into cultural phenomena in Breda North-East. Within the framework of the culture-historical investigation into Breda Noord-East by Steenhuis stedenbouw/landschap and Urban Fabric. With the assistance ofAnneke Abhelakh. Commissioned by the Municipality of Breda, 2008. Pamphlet.

'Van Nachtwacht tot Nachtjacht', concept and supervision of student project for the Arnhem Academy of Architecture. Pamphlet.

'Rechtzaak over de actuele ontwikkelingen in het Nederlandse landschap', concept development and organization in collaboration with Bert van Meggelen. Commissioned by Kasteel Groeneveld. 9 November 2008. With the assistance of Anneke Abhelakh, Kees Vriesman, Dirk Sijmons, Jan Winsemius and others.

2009

'The discovery of the Maasplein', contribution to 'Op Zuid', about the art in Rotterdam-Zuid. Commissioned by the Centrum voor Beeldende Kunst, Rotterdam. With the assistance of Brigitta van Weeren, Dorien Jansen, Els Brouwer and others.
Publication: M. van der Meijden and S.Thissen (eds), *Op Zuid*, Rotterdam 2009 (NAi Publishers), pp 20-25.

'Life, the game', development of a life game from 35 participants for the group exhibition 'Ruhezeit Abgelaufen', curator Hans van Houwelingen, in the Kunstfort Vijfhuizen, Haarlemmermeer. In collaboration with Wouter Baars. With the assistance of Goldfinger (Maxim Chapochnikov) and others. Participants in 'Ruhezeit Abgelaufen' included Rudy Luijters, Ronald Ophuis and Berend Strik.

'Bakens aan de Waal', concept for the role of art and spatial design in processes of spatial transformation along the Waal river. Project plan commissioned by the Cultuurpact Rivierenland/KCG (Conny Verberne and Jeroen de Jong). With the assistance of Els Brouwer, Anneke Abhelakh, Martine Herman and others. Pamphlet.

TtOM, establishment of the Interval Development Company. With Hans Jungerius and Edwin Verdurmen. Discontinued in 2010.

'GastGastgeber' ('Guest Host'), development and implementation of a unifying project for the Dutch contributions

to RUHR.2010. Commissioned by the Consulte General of the Netherlands in Düsseldorf, Germany. With support from the Ministry of OCW and Dutch Design Fashion Architecture. Concept development: Hans Venhuizen, Lucas Verweij and Boris Sieverts. Elaboration in collaboration with KIT e.V.-Oberhausen, Medienbunker-Marxloh, THS-Dortmund, Diakonie-Dortmund, Observatorium-Rotterdam, NL-RUHR-Düsseldorf, RUHR.2010-Essen. With the assistance of Els Brouwer, Jet Christiaanse, Katja Otrupcak and others. Contributors included Jurgen Bey, Judith ter Haar and Gilian Schrofer.

'The Making Of', application of concept development and debate game for the City of Almere, NewTown Institute, WOONBRON (in collaboration with Observatorium and Michaela Stegerwald), Centrum voor Beeldende Kunst Noord-Holland, Municipality of Wieringermeer, the Ministry of VROM, Landschapsbeheer Nederland, MAB Vastgoed, Ymere, and others.

2010

Publication: H. Venhuizen, 'Van laboratoriumjas naar planspel', in: *Nova Terra*, The Hague 2010 (NIROV/Ministry of VROM), February, pp 39-42. A special edition of Randstad 2040.

Publication: 'De essentiële marge', in: S. Lindemann and I. Schutten (eds), *Stedelijke transformatie in de Tussentijd Transvaal, Den Haag*, Amsterdam 2010 (SUN-Trancity), pp 169-178, 189-192.

Publication: H. Venhuizen, 'Muntpark', in: Urban Pilots (eds), *Muntpark: De verborgen schat aan Utrecht*, Utrecht, 2010, pp 43-43. Publication about the transformation of the Utrecht Muntsluis area.

Publication: H. Venhuizen, 'Het Verdronken Land van Lent', in: *Lentereiland*, Nijmegen 2010, pp 60-65. Publication about the transformation of the foreland of the river Waal near Lent, City of Nijmegen.

'The Making Of', application of concept development and debate game for Centrum Beeldende Kunst Utrecht, Ministry of VROM, Municipality of Enschede and others.

'Legenda', foundation of 'Die Gesellschaft für explorative Landeskunde LEGENDA' in Duisburg, Germany. In collaboration with Boris Sieverts, Mustafa Tazeoglu, Dirk Haas and Hans Jungerius.

NOTE OF APPRECIATION

My work comes about on the strength of frequent and often intensive collaboration with many people. The list below contains the names of individuals, firms, government agencies and other bodies that, in one way or another, have contributed to the realization of my projects. They were responsible for the organization of parts of projects or contributed to them; they wrote or translated texts; they designed brochures, websites and catalogues; they carried out research, offered advice, made presentations and proposals or supported them in one way or another. First of all I want to thank those people who made a major contribution to the development or realization of my work, some of them through direct or indirect support, and others through making a concrete contribution. Some of them are perhaps unaware of the importance of their contribution, but I nonetheless wish to extend a particular thanks to: Margit Schuster, Wigger Bierma, Bert van Meggelen, Lucas Verweij, John Körmeling, Wim Korvinus, Bas Maters, Barbara Mayreder, Marcel Smink, Francien van Westrenen, Max Daniel, and of course Jan, Luc, Ellen, and André Venhuizen.

In addition, I am indebted to (in no particular order): Anja Köppchen, Dorien Jansen, Afshan Ayar, Mariëtte Maaskant, Gerrit Kersten, Gerke Veenboer, Isabel van der Zande, Inge Hoonte, Iris van der Vos, Wiebe de Ridder, Marieke Berkers, Saskia Hermanek, Caroline Wolf, Maureen Timmermans, Irmin Eggens, Margot Lieftinck, Nicky Nghuyen, Hilde de Bruijn, Johanne Luhmann, Sytze Malda, Marlene Pinaud, Gracia Khouw, Robin Kolleman, Brigitta van Weeren, Anneke Abhelakh, Els Brouwer, Arjan Raatgever, Joris Maltha & Daniel Gross, ArchiNed, Anniek Brattinga, Victor Joseph, Andrew May, Frank Hemeltjen, Alko de Vries, Jan Brand, Thea van den Heuvel, Peter Frank van der Kooi, Heleen Lamers, Blue Brother and Christiaan Michels, Pieter Becks, Antonio Carrocio, Angelique van Doormalen, Antal Gögös, Rob Groot Zevert, Yaqui Juarez, Sandra van Karssen, Robbert Köppens, Martijn Loosens, Eric Lucas, Jana van Meerveld, Gustavo Restuccia, Renée Smit, Dirk Schreuders, Martin Timmers, Zhera Topaluglu, Bastiaan Visser, Tilo Weber, Arjan Isendoorn, Raoul Bunschoten, Wim Nijenhuis, Mirjam Bakker, Bureau B+B, Rik van Dolderen, Alfred Eikelenboom, Richard Hendrikse & Fred Kapelle, Martine Herman, Germa Huybers, Renato Kindt, Caroline Kortenhorst, Mirjam Kuitenbrouwer, Ton van der Laaken, Erik van Maarschalkerwaard, Kas Oosterhuis & Ilona Lénárd, Ady Steketee, Jerome Symons, Raoul Teulings, Veugen & Veugen, Marius van Workum, Jan van IJzendoorn, Stichting Artibus Sacrum Arnhem, Netherlands Foundation for Visual Arts, Design and Architecture, Joke Ketel, Frank Havermans, Carolina Agelink, Marjon Gemmeke, Karel van der Eijk, Job Saltzherr, Noor de Rooij, Marion Fritz-Jobse, Ineke Middag, Eutopia Potsdam, Jean Hendriks, Jaap van den Born, Volker Oelschläger, Christin Lau, Martin Terpstra, Jacqueline Tellinga, Arjen Mulder, Maaike Post, NBKS, Maarten van Wesemael, Buro Schie, Ad Habets, Frans Sturkenboom, Jean Paul Kerstens, Stichting Undercover, Tom Frantzen (TARRA architectuur & stedenbouw), Geert Bosch and Annemariken Hilberink (Hilberink Bosch architecten), Wies Sanders, Bart Lootsma, NL Architects, Jan van Grunsven, Carel Weeber, Jaap Huisman, Bouchaib Dihaj, Mustapha Driouach, Mark Linnemann, Sjaak de Keijzer, Luuk Kortekaas, Harold Strak, Ewout Dorman, Crimson, Elisabeth Groot, Herman van Bakel, Evelien van Vugt, Lilian Roosenboom, residents of Gouda, Municipality of Gouda, Stimuleringsfonds voor Architectuur, Anjerfonds Zuid-Holland, Kunstgebouw, Rijswijk, de Veemvloer, Amarant Tilburg, Het Praktijkbureau, Albert Koolma, Don van Grunsven, Mariska Noordik, Paul Dekker, Van Helvoirt Groenprojecten, Louis Gijzen, Joop Meijssen, Jan Grave, Wilma Grave, Joseph van de Poel, Sylvie v.d. Vleuten, Huub Slaats, Jorien Michielsen, Piet Graveleyn, Roger Verpoorten, Paul Vanermen, Mondriaan Stichting, Province of Noord-Brabant, Dennis Moet, MG Architecten, Future Lifestyle Innovators, Martijn Schoots, Van Velzen La Feber Bonneur Architecten, Juliette van der Meijden, Henk de Vroom, Toshikazu Ishida (Kyushu JP), Krijn Giezen, Oscar Rommens, Joris van Reusel, Mauricio Corbalan, Gustavo Dieguez, Mark Mantingh, Mark van Steenbergen, Michiel Parqui, Dennis Martens, Cees-Jan de Rooi, Joop Schaghen, Sander van Veen, Connie Eggink, Klaas Hoekstra, Karel Winterink, Sonja Ammerlaan, Esther van Winden, Maria Neele, Pieta Koopman, Wim de Bruijne, Henze Pegman, Carree Comunicatie, Rotterdam, Indira van 't Klooster, Martijn Engelbregt, Nationaal Dubo Centrum, mr. H. Heemrood, J. Warners, H. Lenderink, Paul Berends, Sim Vissers, Harry Harsema, Grafisch Atelier Wageningen, Architectuur Lokaal, NUVORM, ZEE, Parthesius Vormgeving, Werkplaats Vincent de Rijk, Anne Bousema, T. Bijshuizen, Stefan Werrer, Petra Koenen, NAi Publishers, Bergen Arkitekt Skole (Norway), Fachhochschule Biel/Bern (Switzerland), University of Warsaw (Poland), Kunstacademie Arnhem (OK5, Beeldende Kunst en de Publieke Ruimte), Patrick-Henri Burgaud, Heitor Frugoli Junior, Sjaak Langenberg, Annet Delfgauw, Jan Jongert, Denis Oudendijk and Césare Peeren (2012Architecten), Endre Sten Nilsen, residents and various conversation partners within the Municipality of Beuningen, Municipality of Beuningen, Province of Gelderland, Bouwfonds Cultuurfonds, Prins Bernhard Cultuurfonds, VSBfonds, Steven Venhuizen, Beeldleveranciers, Marleen Oud, Olivier Scheffer, Amsterdams Fonds voor de Kunst, Bug Design, Harold Schouten, Mirjam Terpstra, Paul Meyer, Zeger Woudenberg, Lucas van Herwaarden, Lex van Langen, Jacques Stoop, Paul Chin, Bejamin Foerster-Baldenius, Matthias Rick, Marjet van Hartskamp, Municipality of Nieuwegein, Boris Sieverts, Hans van Houwelingen, The Good Guys, Govert Grosfeld, Liesbeth Melis, Ruyter/Roelvink ontwerpers, Bas Vijn, Martine van Kampen, Hans Wesseling, Hetty Bouwhuis, Saskia Flesch, Baldwin Henderson and Iris Casteren van Cattenburgh, Meetkundige Dienst Rijkswaterstaat, Iris Oelschlaeger, UrbanPlan Berlin, residents of Berlijn-Marzahn, Dieuwertje Komen, Saskia Visser, Emma Gossink, S.M.A.M. Venhuizen, Martin Leclercq, Alessa van de Goor, Anne-Marie Veldkamp, Jeanette van Dijk, Chris Koens, Sofie van Westrenen, Geijskes, Rijkent Lamain, Merijn Groenhart, Werkgroep Maak Mheenpark Mooi, Actiegroep Behoud Mheenpark, Wijkraad, Stichting Wisselwerk, residents of Apeldoorn-Zevenhuizen, Erfgoedhuis Zuid-Holland, Onno Helleman, Peter Sevens, Gerda Zijlstra, David Lingerak, Kummer & Herrman, Daan Binnendijk, Maurits Klaren, Sjaak Smakman, Hans Jungerius, Jan Kolen, Geertje Korf, Douwe Sikkema, Frank Helsloot, Jennifer Petterson, Jelle Vervloet, Marc Witteman, Martin Zandwijk, Marca Bultink, Peter Nijhof, Ineke Schwartz, Gert Greveling, Cor van der Heijden, Joop Zwetsloot, Margreet Aangeenbrug, Ton Cats, Karola Dierichs, Cees Freeke, Rudi Halewijn, Johannes Langeveld, Margret van Leeuwen, Jan van Nieuwkoop, Henk van Os, Tjeerd Scheffer, Mark Tilli, Christina Wallone, Bert Wolthuis, Alex de Vries, Stern/Den Hartog & De Vries, Ceciel Oud, SRO, BAVO, Gideon Boie and Matthias Pauwels, Catherine Visser (DaF-architecten), Jan Vaessen, Nathalie de Vries, Dirk Sijmons, Marinus Houtman, Herman Verkerk and Paul Kuipers (Eventarchitectuur), Museum de Zwarte Tulp, Lisse, Annemiek Rijckenberg, Zef Hemel, Pact van Teylingen, Projectsubsidies Belvedere, H. Geerlings,

G. Peeters, BEYOND (projectbureau Leidsche Rijn), BOVAG, RAI, Mariette Dölle, Trudy Timmerman, Rob Hendriks, Erik Leisink, Wijkcentrum Leidsche Rijn, Wijkservicecentrum Vleuten-De Meern, Walter Prigge, Cor Wagenaar, Joost Volkers, Bruno Post, Jan Kadijk, Knooppunt Arnhem-Nijmegen, Dienst Landelijk Gebied, Municipality of Overbetuwe, Municipality of Lingewaard, Jessica Nielsen, Cor Geluk (Juurlink+ Geluk), René van der Velden and Saline Verhoeven (1:1 Stadslandschappen), Florian Boer, -scape, Marco Vermeulen (Urban Affairs), Sylvia Karres and Jan Martijn Eekhof (Karres en Brands), Corine van de Broek, Jeremy Jansen, Yvo Zijlstra and Marcel van der Zwet (Antenna-Men), Marc Laman, Willem Venhuizen, Anne Sevens, Hanne Hagenaars, Marjan Teunissen, Thea de Langen, Rob van Iterson, Marleen van Ooststroom, Karin Tabacnik, Marinke Steenhuis and Paul Meurs (Steenhuis stedenbouw/landschap), Patrick McCabe (REDscape, Landscape and Urbanism), Piet Snellaars, Minke Themans, Brenda Vonk Noordegraaf, Ineke and Sigurdur Gudmundsson (Chinese European Art Centre, Xiamen), Municipality of Elst, Bart Goedbloed, Eduard Kögel, Rudy Stroink, Rients Dijkstra, BVR, Sjoerd Cusveller, Tanja Reith, Hunter Douglas, Willemijn Lofvers, Jacques Abelman, Rianne Makkink, Sloom.org, Wim Timmermans, Esther Didden, Sabrina Lindemann, Iris Schutten, Linlin, Jiawen Hou, Landy, Song Chi, Guohaipeng, Johnson, Mark van der Wegen, Erik-Jan Mans, Annemarie van den Berg, André Dekker, Ruud Reutelingsperger, Geert van de Camp, Observatorium, Leo van Loon, Netherlands Architecture Institute, CBKU, Ella Derksen, Annelou Evelein, Tom van Gestel, Ton Verstegen, Martijn Duineveld, Kees Vriesman, Jan Winsemius, Jan Hartholt, M. van der Meijden, Siebe Thissen, Wouter Baars, DJ Goldfinger (Maxim Chapochnikov), Kim Knoppers, Martijntje van Schooten, Conny Verberne, Jeroen de Jong, KCG, Edwin Verdurmen, Consulaat Generaal der Nederlanden in Düsseldorf, Inez Boogaarts, Felix Eich, Christine de Baan, Carlie Janszen, Hester Swaving, Ingeborg van Lieshout, Bart Hofstede, Ellen Klaus, Esther Agricola, Gabor Freivogel, Henk van der Veen, Hu jia, Huib Haye van der Werf, Jaap van Dijk, Jan Samsom, Jandirk Hoekstra, Jerry Remkes, Karin van Pinxteren, Katja Assman, Jan Konings, Lina Lau, Linde Egberts, Macha Roesink, Marina van Bergen, Markus Ambach, Martin del Peco, Jaap Modder, Maike van Stiphout, Linda Vlassenrood, Wilfried Lentz, Xin Xia, Ministry of Education, Culture and Science, Dutch Design Fashion Architecture, KIT e.V.-Oberhausen, Medienbunker-Marxloh, THS-Dortmund, Diakonie-Dortmund, NL-RUHR-Düsseldorf, RUHR.2010-Essen, Jet Christiaanse, Katja Otrupcak, Jurgen Bey, Judith ter Haar, Gilian Schrofer, Michaela Stegerwald, Centrum voor Beeldende Kunst Noord-Holland, Municipality of Wieringermeer, Ministry of Housing, Spatial Planning and the Environment, Landschapsbeheer Nederland, MAB Vastgoed, Ymere, Henk Ovink, Bart Vink, Saskia Newrly, David ter Avest, Tom Maas, Urban Pilots, Henri van der Vegt, Allard Koers, P.M. van Wijk, Gertjan Venhuizen, Karin van Leeuwen, Municipality of Enschede, Mustafa Tazeoglu, Ed Annink, Marc Neelen, Arie Lengkeek, Patrick van der Klooster, Billie Erlenkamp, Eric Dil, Dirk Haas, and everyone I have forgotten to mention.

INDEX

COLOPHON

Author: Hans Venhuizen
and Charles Landry, Francien van
Westrenen
Translation Dutch-English
(all texts, except Landry): Billy Nolan
Translation English-Dutch (Landry):
Leo Reijnen
Compilation: Hans Venhuizen, Francien
van Westrenen, Astrid Vorstermans
Image editing: Bureau Venhuizen with
Meeus Ontwerpt
Images: (Bureau) Hans Venhuizen,
unless otherwise stated
Graphic design: Meeus Ontwerpt,
Hilde & Janna Meeus, with thanks to
Wigger Bierma
Copy-editing: Els Brinkman
Printing: Die Keure, Bruges (B)
Publisher: Valiz, Amsterdam

©Valiz, book and cultural projects; Hans
Venhuizen; authors and photographers, 2010
All rights reserved.

Distribution:
NL/BE/LU: Coen Sligting,
www.coensligtingbookimport.nl; Centraal
Boekhuis, www.centraalboekhuis.nl;
Scholtens, www.scholtens.nl
GB/IE: Art Data, www.artdata.co.uk
Europe/Asia: Idea Books,
www.ideabooks.nl
USA: D.A.P. www.artbook.com

ISBN 979-90-78088-46-2 (E)
NUR 648

This publication is also available in a
Dutch edition:
Hans Venhuizen, *Game Urbanism
Handleiding voor een culturele ruimtelijke
ordening*
ISBN Dutch edition: 978-90-78088-30-1 (N)

www.valiz.nl

BUREAU VENHUIZEN
www.bureauvenhuizen.com

**Credits of the images, photographs
Hans Venhuizen, unless otherwise
stated:**
Cover - Parquette in Museum
De Paviljoens in Almere, 2008.
Photo Gert Jan van Rooij
P 38 Shopping mall under construction,
Xiamen, China.
P 39 Karlsaue during Documenta 12,
Kassel, Germany.
P 44 Fake wooden bridge in Xiamen,
China.
P 45 New traditional garden in Songjiang,
China.
P 52 Landschaftspark Duisburg-Nord,
Duisburg, Germany.
P 53 Margarethenhöhe, Essen, Germany.
P 60 Market in Kuala Lumpur, Malaysia.
P 61 B20 at Berchtesgaden, Germany.
P 70 Zsolnay-area in Pécs, Hungary.
P 71 Huandao East Road in Xiamen,
China.
P 78 Piercing shop Ostbahnhof, Berlin,
Germany.
P 79 Toy shop Mid Valley megamall, Kuala
Lumpur, Malaysia.
P 86 Herdenkingsplein, Maastricht,
the Netherlands.
P 87 Historic new developments in
Ningbo, China.
P 92 Bonsai seller in São Paulo, Brazil.
P 93 Garden in Ningbo, China.
P 100 Break for the Teletubbie man in
Kiev, the Ukraïne.
P 101 Political babouschka's on the cen-
tral market, Budapest, Hungary.
Photo Margit Schuster
P 108 Spring after the sandstorm in
Beijing, China.
P 109 Camouflage tree in Budapest,
Hungary.

Illustrations in the margin of pages
42 - 46 - 48 - 49 - 50 - 56 - 57 (based on
the work of prize winners and on the
elaboration of project **BULB & BREAKFAST**, a
competition as part of **SOUL AND SOIL**, 2004)
**- 58 - 62 - 64 - 65 - 67 - 68 - 72 - 74 - 76 - 77 -
80 - 81 - 83 - 84 - 88 - 90 - 91 - 99 - 102 - 104 -
110 - 112** made by Brigitta van Weeren for
Bureau Venhuizen.

The author and the publisher have made
every effort to secure permission to
reproduce the listed material - illustrations and photographs. We apologize for
any inadvert errors or omissions. Parties
who nevertheless believe they can claim
specific legal rights are invited to contact
the publisher: info@valiz.nl.

This publication was made possible
through the generous support of

The Netherlands Architecture Fund
and HGIS

The Netherlands Foundation for Visual
Arts, Design and Architecture

With many thanks to:
Museum De Paviljoens, Almere

Printed and bound in Belgium